SHOULD STUDENTS SHARE THE POWER?

A Study of Their Role in
College and University Governance

Earl J. McGrath

Foreword by Martin Meyerson

TEMPLE UNIVERSITY PRESS
Philadelphia 1970

Standard Book Number 87722-003-4
Library of Congress Card Number 70-133135
Printed in the United States of America
Copyright © 1970 by Earl J. McGrath
All Rights Reserved

Contents

Foreword, by Martin Meyerson   1
Introduction   3

Background   9

HISTORY AND PRESENT PRACTICE   9
The Early Student and the Faculty Guilds   10
*The Passing of Student Control and the Rise of
    Paternalism*   13
Unformalized Student Powers   17

INDIRECT STUDENT INFLUENCE   19
Antioch's Long and Successful Experience   22
Changes in Academic Government in Canada   31

A SURVEY OF EXISTING PRACTICE   38
Students on Boards of Trustees   39

For and Against Student Participation   51

RATIONALE FOR STUDENT PARTICIPATION   51
Institutional Professions and Actions   51
The Sophistication of Students Today   52
Students Should Be Educated for Democratic Living   53
Students Could Help Improve Higher Education   54
The Abolition of the Doctrine of In Loco Parentis   56
The Improvement of Instruction   57

OBJECTIONS TO STUDENT PARTICIPATION   60
Students Will Dominate the Academic Society   60
The Immaturity of Students   62
The Brief Involvement of Students   63

Ignorance of Professional Values   64
Interference with Study and Gainful Employment   65

SUMMARY   66

Techniques for Achieving Student Participation   72

Abolition of the Term "Student Government"   72

PRACTICAL PROBLEMS OF STUDENT PARTICIPATION   74
Proportion of Student Membership   74
    The background of experience   79
Method of Selection of Student Representatives   79
    Student rejection of elected representatives   80
Voting Rights for Students   81
    Proportionate representation   82

RESTRUCTURING ACADEMIC GOVERNMENT   84
The Academic Society, Community of Learning   84
The "Accountability" Theory   86
A Modified Tripartite Form of Government   89
The Advancement of Education   92

SPECIFIC PREPARATION FOR GOVERNMENTAL SERVICES   93

ENABLING STUDENTS TO PARTICIPATE   96

THE USE OF REASON IN ACADEMIC REFORM   100

Conclusions   103

Appendix   106

STUDENT PARTICIPATION IN SELECTED POLICY-MAKING
    BODIES OF COLLEGES AND UNIVERSITIES: FIVE TABLES
1. *Overall*   106
2. *By Highest Level of Institutional Offering*   108
3. *By Institutional Enrollment, 1967-68*   110
4. *By Type of Institutional Support*   112
5. *By Accrediting Region*   114

Bibliography   116

Foreword

It is widely supposed that students participate today in the governance of colleges and universities to an unprecedented degree. Perhaps this is the case. But there is a critical lack of information of two sorts behind such a supposition: first, historical material on the extent of student participation at earlier periods in the United States and in other countries; and second, reliable data about the character of current student participation in American college and university governance.

A few rather sketchy surveys were conducted in the mid-1950's. Not surprisingly, they concluded that students of the silent generation accepted a virtual exclusion from the governance of the institutions at which they studied. Then, for a decade and a half, almost nothing was known —nor even sought—about the degree of student participation. Indeed, the study of all facets of university government languished, so that the recent waves of concern caught those involved in American higher education with pathetically poor information about the relative roles of various constituencies.

At various points in his long and distinguished career as an observer of higher education, Earl McGrath has focused attention on neglected subjects. As professor, dean and head of a college, as United States Commissioner of Education and most especially as director of the higher education centers at Columbia and at Temple, he has filled serious gaps in our knowledge of university governance. His works have, moreover, spurred the scholarship of others.

Therefore, we should hardly be surprised to find the current question of the students' stake in university governance to be the theme of Dr. McGrath's most recent study. But the genesis of the study, and its special relationship to the Assembly on University Goals and Governance, affiliated with the American Academy of Arts and Sciences, merit mention. When the Assembly began its work in September 1969, Dr. McGrath had already developed for foundation support an outline of a survey of student participation, the results of which are reported in this essay. Because of close parallels between his interests and those of the five policy councils within the Assembly, it seemed appropriate that the two efforts should be linked. The survey results have illuminated important aspects of the Assembly, and in particular the inquiry of the Assembly's Policy Council on Models of Governance into the changing relations among university constituencies.

Much more remains to be done. Dr. McGrath himself plans an expanded analysis of many questions that have emerged during this survey. His essay marks an important way station along a path the future course of which is uncertain and probably tortuous for all of us in higher education.

Martin Meyerson, Chairman
The Assembly on University
Goals and Governance

Introduction

Few periods in American history have seen more radical and swift modification of social institutions than our own. A reexamination of traditional purposes, programs, and procedures is now the order of the day in the church, in government, in industry, and indeed in all social organizations. The age-old ways of doing things are under searching and unrestrained scrutiny. Under present circumstances it is not surprising that the policies and practices of educational institutions should be subjected to review and that basic change should be proposed.

All through the history of American higher education there have been sporadic efforts at reform, and sometimes students have been deeply involved in such activities; but these efforts have generally been short in life and modest in results. Now students are strongly advocating changes in society at large and modifications of academic policies and practices related to these changes. In several respects the interests and activities of present-day college and university students differ from those of their predecessors.

The involvement of students today is more general in the country at large, and the number of young people on individual campuses is typically larger than hitherto. Some have contended that the percentage of students directly involved in reform activities is negligible. While it is true that the proportion of hard-core activists is relatively small, the number concerned about the resolution of our persistent economic, political, and social problems and the reform of educational conventions is considerable. Moreover, the students' interests are more deep-seated and lasting.

In respect to the subject treated in this volume, however, today's students differ most significantly from earlier generations in their awareness that there is a direct relationship between the character and quality of higher education and social policy and practice. Whatever other beneficial results they expect from higher education, they are convinced that it ought to play a major role in the improvement of the human enterprise. Many students today see a great gap between the actual and the potential contributions of institutions of higher education to their own well-being and to society.

Students also recognize that however committed the members of the society of learning may be to the pursuit of new knowledge, as a group they are singularly uninterested in a critical examination of the practices of the establishment and firmly disinclined to change them. Consequently, many students believe that if any significant reforms in educational objectives and procedures are to be accomplished, the conventional government of institutions must be so altered as to give students an influential role in the formulation of institutional policies. They exhibit a widespread interest in academic reform. It is a fair prediction that even if other external social issues of war, race, and pollution decline in urgency, students, as many have already done, will turn their attention to the steps which need to be taken to gain a more influential place in academic government. Even if pressing social problems are not resolved or mitigated, students may in angry frustration make more vigorous and insistent demands for a part in bringing the activities of institutions of higher education into more effective relationship with the life of their time. Student participation in academic government is quite unlikely to turn out to be a passing fad.

Until recently there has been no comprehensive body of fact with respect to the actions of colleges and universities in admitting students to their policy-making bodies. Moreover, the literature treating the theoretical issues related to student involvement has generally been unsystematic, fragmentary, and fugitive. Yet the interest in this subject is widespread not only among those directly involved in higher education, but among the public at large. Recognizing the need for a comprehensive review of existing practice and a position statement on the issues inherent in student participation in governance, the American Academy of Arts and Sciences engaged the author to make a study of existing practices, to gather opinions on their effectiveness, and to make such proposals concerning desirable policies as experience and reason seemed to support. This volume is intended to report on the execution of this mission.

The primary data which constitute the factual basis of generalizations concerning institutional practices as of the end of 1969 were supplied by the presidents of colleges and universities listed in the directory of the United States Office of Education. Over 900 replies were received, of which only a few, for one reason or another, were unusable. In addition to being requested for data which could be treated statistically, such as the number and kinds of faculty committees to which students had been admitted, presidents were asked to express opinions concerning the theoretical value of student participation and its practical success in their institutions. Since the universities and colleges of Canada had made such extensive study of this matter and had instituted many promising innovations, their presidents were also included in the inquiry. From all these sources a vast body of fact and opinion with respect to present practice was collected, classified, and collated.

Added to the gathering of these direct reports was an extensive survey of the literature on the subject. In comparison with other common educational topics, the subject of student participation was discovered to be inconspicuous. In fact some of the most valuable and realistic statements consisted of reports prepared by institutional committees largely for internal use. In any event an effort was made to examine any available written expression of opinion. Also, numerous conversations were held with persons who either had considered the theoretical implications of student involvement or had undertaken the difficult task of working with various institutional groups such as trustees, administrators, faculty members, or students in the revision of existing governmental structures.

The author believes that the facts and opinions reported represent the current situation as accurately as is humanly possible. Since events in academic communities today move with unprecedented swiftness, the summary figures on existing practice may have changed within the six-month period from the gathering of the data to the publication of the findings. A casual review of such additional information as has appeared in recent weeks, however, suggests that in August 1970 students have become more extensively involved in academic government than they were at the beginning of the year 1969-70. All available evidence suggests that this trend will accelerate in 1970-71, and with growing experience more reliable judgments will be possible concerning the validity of various policies and practices. The evidence also clearly indicates, however, that those who wish to stabilize institutional life and capitalize on the assets of student commitment and dedicated effort will no longer dissipate energy in debating whether students should or should not have a role in academic governance. That question has been answered by developments on the campuses and in society at large. The primary consideration at this time is how students can be most effectively involved in deliberative and legislative bodies. This report is calculated to assist those involved in academic reconstruction by providing a body of related practical experience and theoretical discussion.

The author wishes to express his gratitude to the officers of the American Academy of Arts and Sciences, especially to Dr. Martin Meyerson, who made this study possible and who gave valuable advice and criticism along the way. The hundreds of college and university presidents and others who undertook the increasingly irritating task of filling out questionnaires and answering additional inquiries merit a special expression of thanks. Sidney Letter and Josephine Yankauskas of the staff of the Temple Higher Education Center were diligent and efficient in analyzing the data and in preparing the manuscript for printing.

In the last pages the reader will find in addition to a series of statistical tables an extensive bibliography prepared in the first instance by the author, but considerably augmented by a related list of readings entitled "Student Participation in Academic Governance," issued by the ERIC (Educational Resources Information Center) Clearinghouse on Higher Education. Those who wish to study various aspects of student participation intensively will find the ERIC list especially helpful because of its subject classifications and its incisive annotations. The author wishes to express his thanks to Dr. Carl J. Lange of The George Washington University for the privilege of using the list of readings prepared under the auspices of his organization.

JB Lon Hefferlin, of the Ellis Phillips Foundation, made valuable criticisms of the manuscript which resulted in a better organization and a more lucid presentation of the material.

In these days when long delays in publishing have become the practice rather than the exception, it is a pleasure to acknowledge the expeditious help of Temple University Press in producing this publication in little more than a month.

August 1, 1970   Earl J. McGrath

BACKGROUND

HISTORY AND PRESENT PRACTICE

The history of higher education does not supply much instruction to those who today seek to determine the proper role of students in academic government. Except for several centuries at the very beginning of the Italian universities and the past fifty years in the United States, students have not had any formal place in the governmental structure. A cursory review of the organic development of universities will, however, reveal one significant fact that might encourage open-mindedness among those who try to reconstruct the government of American colleges and universities.

Since the rise of the University of Bologna, nine centuries ago, institutions of higher education have been composed of three major social groups—trustees, faculty members, and students. Although these constituents have at different times gone by various names such as governors, masters, and scholars, the modern tripartite classification suitably defines and distinguishes them. The historical fact that lends perspective to the present discussions is that each of

9

these groups has at some time dominated the academic community and under the prevailing circumstances managed it with reasonable effectiveness.

The Early Student and the Faculty Guilds

In the earliest university societies in Italy the students controlled all aspects of corporate life except the processes which the members of the teaching profession used to recruit its initiates. The university was a privately established guild, created by students. As Rashdall, the celebrated medievalist, observes:

> To appreciate the fact that the university was in its origins nothing more than a guild of foreign students is the key to the real origin and nature of the institution. . . . Thus the evidence all points to the conclusion that the earliest *universitas* of students originated with the foreign students of Bologna in the course of the last quarter of the twelfth century.[1]

The concept of the *universitas,* the term then used, was not at all cognate to the modern university; the word merely meant all of a group. It applied only to the student populations and did not include the teachers, or doctors, as they were later called. After abandoning their position as independent entrepreneurs the teachers formed their own corporate structure, known as a *collegium.* Like the *universitas,* the *collegium* was a guild, a society of masters, organized largely to protect its members against students,

[1] Hastings Rashdall, *The Universities of Europe in the Middle Ages* (London: Oxford University Press, 1936), vol. 1, pp. 161-62.

citizens, and civic authorities. In sharp contrast with its faculty counterparts today, the *collegium* had little authority over educational policies and practices, and virtually no parietal control over the lives of students. In fact the present faculty-student relationships in policy formation are a diametrical reversal of their medieval antecedents. Then the students, through the official acts of the *universitas* and through their own elected executive officer, the rector, imposed rigid controls over the teacher's professional activities and indeed over his community relationships. They prescribed the hours when the teacher should meet his classes, the character of the lectures, the scheduling and the content of his examinations, the amount of his compensation, and the times when he could be absent not only from the classroom but from the town as well.

The single right unequivocally reserved to the professors, a prerogative which nearly a millennium later they still jealously guard, reserved to the *collegium* the privilege of determining its own membership through a rigid examination of the supplicants for admission. Through this device of screening those who sought to teach, the guild of masters maintained a modest indirect control over the general personal acceptability of its members, the subject matter they professed, their methods of instruction, and the place of their residence. In the character of their organization and the fealty required of members, the fraternity of masters duplicated other guilds founded for protection and mutual benefit. Applicants who passed the prerequisite examinations, including a public discourse, were accepted into the *collegium* and at Bologna given the title of doctor of civil or canon law. In time this group formed a body of men who possessed a virtual monopoly of the learning of their day, constituting an organization which formed an effective counterbalance to student power.

But as Rashdall observes, the *universitas,* as contrasted with the *collegium,* for several centuries exercised almost all-encompassing power:

> The combined force of the social and the spiritual penalties thus wielded by the guilds was so enormous that in the Italian cities they often became more powerful than the State. At Bologna the revolution of 1228 gave them an important constitutional position; their magistrates were almost equal in authority to the magistrates of the republic and almost independent of their control.[2]

Thus, since the guilds of students enjoyed most of the privileges and the strength of the municipal government, they amounted to a *civitas in civitate.* The early attempts of the *collegium* to subjugate students by making them a subordinate unit within the guild of doctors rather than an independent profession were abortive. For several centuries the protests of the teachers went unheeded while the power of the students' guilds grew, always sustained by their threat of a boycott of recalcitrant professors or of an emigration from an offending city.

The history of these earliest corporate structures in Western higher education shows that under certain circumstances they were capable of controlling and operating institutions of advanced learning. It also supplies evidence that different social circumstances produce different kinds of government. In terms of later events it indicates that organizations functioning well within one ecology become ineffective in another. Bologna exhibits features of academic life

[2] Rashdall, vol. 1, p. 153.

which few if any advocates of academic reform would find acceptable today. Under the prevailing academic government membership in the student guild was rigidly limited, the administration was imperious, the faculty suffered unconscionable restraints in their professional and personal lives, and the scholastic and civic communities were separate and often contending social organizations. Moreover, the scholastic body politic was composed predominantly of men of mature age and prominent families, who had achieved wealth or status in the community, the church, or the state. In brief, they were men of affairs accustomed to shaping and directing important enterprises. Obviously the Bolognese academic structure, whatever its merits, cannot serve as an acceptable prototype for American higher education in 1970.

The Passing of Student Control and the Rise of Paternalism

In view of the social development at the end of the medieval period, it is not surprising that student control did not survive. In time the masters, resenting student dominance, joined with various outside non-academic authorities, the town officials, the church, and eventually the king, to weaken the students' reign and commensurately to strengthen their own. In order to free themselves from the bondage which financial dependence imposed, the teachers by threat of migration exacted salaries from town officials to take the place of tuition fees. This practice grew in popularity with town officials and professors alike as they recognized in it a device to sap the power of the student guilds. As civic leaders and private donors provided more and more funds to the academic establishment, the influence of these outsiders in the internal policy-making organization grew. The donors increasingly claimed the right to administer their benefactions and to supervise the activities of those who received them. The latter practice gradually led to the official establishment of boards of curators or similar bodies. Rashdall, tracing the history of this shift in control, observes:

> In the course of the fourteenth and fifteenth centuries such a body . . . was established by the city government or prince in all Italian universities, and the real control of the university more and more passed to this body of external governors, which by the sixteenth or seventeenth century succeeded in destroying the student autonomy or reducing it to a shadow.[3]

To all intents and purposes student dominance over academic societies was dead. The students ceased to play any part in academic government or, except as supplicants and petitioners, even to have a minor voice in policy-making processes. For a time then after the fifteenth century the citizens who supported the universities controlled them through official bodies not unlike boards of trustees. In order to keep present-day discussions within the bounds of historical accuracy, it is important to correct a misconception held by many members of the profession to the effect that the American board of trustees is *sui generis*. On the contrary, powerful counterparts of official external boards antedate the founding of our first institution by several centuries, and during this intervening period external supervision and sanction grew and student control declined.

[3] Rashdall, vol. 1, p. 212.

In the course of these centuries still another pattern of government emerged, which placed control in the hands of the professoriate. In the English universities three forces gradually shifted the responsibilities of government from the civil and ecclesiastical to the academic authorities. First, the benefactions of wealthy patrons who made gifts and bequests in perpetuity reduced the need for civic or church support and commensurately increased fiscal independence of the colleges. Second, as the profession of teaching grew in size and influence within the church and state, it became a more cohesive and respected group which could demand greater freedom and self-determination. Third, the students in English universities differed markedly from those in Italian universities. The continental institutions had begun as professional schools training mature practitioners, while the English colleges at Oxford and Cambridge were cloistered preparatory schools tutoring apprentice clerics. Their students were indeed "junior fellows"—younger than their Italian counterparts; they were novices and were expected to emulate the virtues of their elders in both learning and piety. Hence, the leaders of church and state in England considered it entirely proper to turn over power for the internal operation of the colleges to the doctors and masters —the faculty.

The American colonies adopted English educational precedents regarding faculty control of student life, but they did not adopt English precedents regarding faculty control of the institution. Rather than relying on the masters and fellows themselves to be their own trustees and vesting the right of occasional visitation and adjudication in a single outside dignitary, as had the Oxford and Cambridge colleges, the colonial American colleges adopted the Scottish form of academic governance, whereby a group of laymen served as the ultimate governing body for the institution. This model of governance stemmed originally from the Italian universities but more directly from the Reformation universities: Calvin's Academy, Geneva, in 1559, Leyden in 1575, Edinburgh in 1583, and Trinity College, Dublin, in 1591—all of which opened on the Reformation plan of lay control of institutional governance. Thus, for example, neither of Harvard's two governing boards has been dominated by faculty membership, despite a series of faculty attempts, culminating in the 1720's and again in the 1820's, to obtain control of the smaller of the two boards—the seven-man Corporation.

In short, this review of academic government shows that at various stages in the evolution of higher education, control has been held at one time or another by students, by faculty, and by laymen. Through recent years the dominant trend has been the growth of *de facto* power of the faculty over all academic policies, even in institutions putatively governed by laymen and where academic policies have been specifically placed by law in the hands of the lay board. As part of this trend, the power of students has been subordinated. Their role has been that of children—wards of a paternalistic institution, to be disciplined and molded into maturity. Unlike their Bolognese forerunners, who had dominant control over academic establishments, university students of recent centuries have been financially dependent. They have been sent to college by their families or accepted on scholarships; they themselves have not paid the bills. And thus while tensions have periodically erupted about the prerogatives of faculty members and of the lay board, the status of students has remained unchanged. As one group of authors recently put it, students have been the raw material out of which the faculty has made a product. From the establishment of Harvard until today, with only the most atypical exception, the influence of students has been limited to indirect action. They might voice their opinions of their teachers, their courses of study, or the conditions of campus life; they might petition for redress of grievances; they might object to regulations and restrictions; they might foment demonstrations and rebellions; all these things American college and university students have done over the past three centuries. But theirs was the privilege of protest, not of power, and theirs was the duty of obedience, not of participation. In a patriarchal culture and in an autocratic or oligarchic institution, it was unthinkable for students to expect to exert direct influence on educational policies through membership in institutional councils.

Unformalized Student Powers

Although some observers who are shocked at today's campus turmoil may not know it, the history of American higher education has been spotted with student agitation, protest, and subversion: it is a tumultuous record of riots in the dining commons, of the waylaying of unsuspecting tutors, of assaults on punctilious professors, of tortuous collegiate tricks on collegial authority, of sullen student dissatisfaction and boisterous student resentment. "Not every college underwent a rebellion," Frederick Rudolph, the most perceptive of academic historians, has written, "and the rebellions were inspired by a variety of conditions. Generally, however, they took the form of a concerted strike of a majority of the undergraduates, protesting against some real or imagined wrong, threatening to withdraw from the college and to abandon it to the uncertainties of enrollment and finance that were bound to follow."[4]

Into the middle of the nineteenth century American colleges retained their English tradition of cloistered paternalism; and for every whipping they administered, their students could retaliate with obstinacy. But with the trend of American higher education toward German ideals after the Civil War—the goals of scientific research, of graduate instruction, and of intellectual concern rather than pietistic obedience—the existing colleges began to relinquish their severe patriarchal supervision, and the newly arising universities such as Cornell and Johns Hopkins could avoid it almost completely.

As the nineteenth century neared its end, many institutions decided that students might possibly be trusted to select their own courses, to find their own housing, to keep their own hours, to be responsible for themselves. The students began to assume control over their out-of-class lives and to organize their own educational program: the extra-curriculum. If the institutions did not provide opportunities for recreation, the students would organize athletics; if the institutions abandoned their protected and policed dormitories, the students would organize fraternity houses; if the curriculum remained stagnant, the students would pursue unconcernedly such courses as they had to and establish their own scholarly clubs and interest groups.

The influence of this change from the English to the German model of academic life is exemplified at Amherst,

[4] *The American College and University: A History* (New York: Alfred A. Knopf, 1962), p. 97.

where the college delegated to the students authority over questions of student "order and decorum." Amherst's 1880 decision, after large-scale rioting and disobedience, gave the undergraduate body considerable responsibility for the conduct of their own affairs, with the proviso of a presidential veto. Even so, with the exception of the free choice of courses under the elective system, student initiative was limited largely to the social, or non-academic, aspects of the college experience.

"Student government," as it developed almost universally on campuses across the nation, remained entirely extracurricular. The officers of student organizations enjoyed neither the right to nor the responsibility for collaboration with the faculty in determining academic purposes, policies, or practices. They were allowed to concern themselves only with such matters as the scheduling of student activities, the maintenance of honor systems, the holding of elections, and eventually with the securing of speakers in public lecture series and with the editing and producing of a student paper. But more often than not even these activities were subject to review by faculty advisers and administrative officers. Academic policies—the decisions which really determined the character and quality of the students' education—remained the prerogative of their elders.

INDIRECT STUDENT INFLUENCE

It would be erroneous to conclude that in unstructured, *ad hoc,* unofficial ways American college students have not been influential in shaping institutional policies. To the contrary, lacking *de jure* power, students have frequently utilized their *de facto* power of numbers and persistence. They have initiated or supported efforts to introduce into the college curriculum all of the modern disciplines—the modern languages, the sciences, the fine arts, the technologies, and more recently a great range of professional and vocational instruction. Indeed, to Rudolph, they have been "the most creative and imaginative force in the shaping of the American college and university."[5] On occasion they have dramatically influenced the entire academic program —as W. H. Cowley, senior editor of the Dartmouth paper, did in 1925, as Edward C. Aswell and Dolph Cheek did in the 1926 Harvard Student Council study of Harvard education, as Jim Nixon and Mike Volzick did in 1965 with the Experimental College at San Francisco State, and as Ira Magaziner and Elliot Maxwell did in 1967 in Brown University's curricular study.

After the President's Commission on Student Involvement in Decision-Making at Cornell University reviewed the informal influence of students on institutional policy, its chairman concluded in his report:

> . . . although in the past the student has had little opportunity to participate formally in faculty and administrative decisions, his own personal decisions may have effects on the institution greater than generally recognized. For example, as students turn away from majoring in physics or chemistry,

[5] "Neglect of Students as a Historical Tradition," in Lawrence E. Dennis and Joseph F. Kauffman, eds., *The College and the Student* (Washington, D.C.: American Council on Education, 1966), p. 47.

the department will ask itself if it is requiring too heavy a concentration on specialized or uninteresting courses. The increasing tendency of students to work harder and take more advanced courses in high school has already had an important influence on the development of new and presumably better offerings at the college level. If more and more students elect to go into the social sciences, more and more teachers will be hired to help meet the demand, purchases for the library will be turned in this direction, and plans may be made for a new social science building.

Similarly, student preferences in regard to housing and dining influence the choice made by administrators. Many universities, for example, have slowed down dormitory building programs as students have turned more and more to private apartments. . . .[6]

But at these institutions, as at almost every other American college or university, the influence of student leaders and reformers has been occasional, episodic, and informal; and their techniques have been petition, persuasion, and pressure because these were the only kinds of leverage students possessed. Moreover, their efforts were often intractably resisted by the administration and faculty alike; and students, however strong their case may have been in principle, were left without recourse to any legal method to achieve what they considered necessary reforms. Except for a few notable institutional exceptions, American students have played no regularized part in academic government.

[6] Robert S. Morison, *The President's Commission on Student Involvement in Decision-Making: The Chairman's Report* (Ithaca: Cornell University, June 11, 1969), p. 35.

Antioch's Long and Successful Experience

The few exceptions to the practice of limiting student decision-making, covering decades of experience, are of signal significance because they demonstrate that under proper circumstances formal student participation can be vitally and effectively productive. The American institution with the longest tradition and, on the whole, the most satisfactory experience with student enfranchisement is Antioch College, in Yellow Springs, Ohio. Like its counterparts, up until the early 1920's Antioch had a conventional governmental structure composed of a board of trustees, a chief administrative officer, and a faculty, each of which to one degree or another exercised policy-making powers. At that time Antioch's students played no more influential role in decision-making than did their contemporaries elsewhere. By the end of World War I, however, Antioch had fallen on bad days. It had few students, few faculty, and few resources. By 1920 the board, recognizing that vigorous and imaginative leadership was essential to survival, appointed to the presidency Arthur Morgan, an engineer and a man of vision, energy, and imagination, later to become famous as the director of the Tennessee Valley Authority. Through a series of radical reforms that would unquestionably have been vigorously opposed by the members of a more flourishing center of learning, Morgan revitalized the community and the program of Antioch. The college became the "New Antioch" of Morgan.

One of Morgan's ideas about education is particularly germane to this discussion. He believed that colleges ought to use the period of higher education in students' lives to prepare the students for the intelligent discharge of their future civic responsibilities in the larger society. Accordingly, in 1926 the new president, urged by students, persuaded his associates that an elected "community government," not just a "student government," should be formed to govern non-academic and non-corporate matters, that is, community living. In this organization members at Antioch elected from all groups involved in the institution —clerical and custodial employees and students as well as faculty and administration—were to make the general policies for community life. Later Algo Henderson initiated the practice of having the elected student in this community government sit as an observer with the administrative council of the college, an academic body which in the early days merely advised the president. Henderson, at first dean but by 1936 president, confirmed and strengthened this precedent by encouraging the council to take full responsibility for the establishment of policy; and in the early forties he formalized student membership in this body.

The administrative council, which continues to function, now consists of three students elected at large by all members of the community, two faculty members elected at large, and three faculty members elected by the faculty, the dean, and the president, *ex officio*. This body, which still reflects Henderson's democratic philosophy of group action, has responsibility for making all policies affecting curriculum content, teaching practices, admissions standards, graduation requirements, student life, the budget, and the election, promotion, and tenure of faculty members and administrative officers other than the president. In one of his books, President Henderson sets forth his philosophy of student involvement in general and treats policy-making and student participation in particular. He believes that:

The question fundamentally is whether the administration takes all the responsibility for the life of the campus, attempting to regulate the affairs of the students by rules and disciplinary procedures, thus leaving the students free to get by with minimum observance of the rules and gain indirect rewards and satisfactions for disobeying them; or whether, on the other hand, the administration succeeds in placing the responsibility upon the students for attending to many of these things themselves, and challenges them to participate in the formation of a community life that has a healthy tone and is conducive to the achievement of the objectives for which the students came to the institution.[7]

Antioch is by no means the only American institution of higher education that for a number of years has admitted students to full membership in deliberative and legislative bodies. Roosevelt University, founded in 1945, has from the beginning given students a voice in policy-making. It has two students as regular voting members of the university senate, and students sit on many faculty committees. Since its establishment in 1932, Bennington College has involved students in all bodies having responsibility for educational policies and for the general conditions of institutional life. Sarah Lawrence, Marlboro, and Goddard Colleges have likewise made students full members in their policy-making and governing agencies. In the current debates concerning the merits of student participation, it is important to remember that on none of these campuses would a majority or even any substantial number of students or staff members advocate exchanging present inclusive policy-making bodies for the more conventional governmental structures in which students have no place.

[7] *Policies and Practices in Higher Education* (New York: Harper and Brothers, 1960), p. 234.

The involvement of students at these atypical institutions inevitably stirs up certain questions concerning (1) the origins of their practices, (2) the reasons why other institutions generally have not adopted such practices, and (3) the possible usefulness of these unusual patterns of governance as models for comparable developments elsewhere. Specifically, why in the 1920's, when students in the higher education enterprise at large had no voice whatever in the formulation of academic policy, was Antioch able to inaugurate a set of broadly democratic procedures? This query requires a multifaceted answer. In the first place, the administrative leaders were men of innovative vision and firm conviction. Morgan and Henderson, and their successors as well, had a well-conceived philosophy of education which they articulated with such skill and sincerity that it drew the support of their associates. The history of American higher education reveals that, regardless of their varied educational ideals, the vision, conviction, and energy of such men as Eliot at Harvard, Harper at Chicago, Butler at Columbia, and Gilman at Johns Hopkins were largely instrumental in bringing to national eminence the institutions over which these men presided. So it was at Antioch. A thoughtful and inspired leadership, in which student involvement constituted only one element, was the dominant factor in the development there.

Yet there were men of comparable qualities in sister institutions, large and small, some of whom saw the merits of many features of the Antioch plan. Why, then, after years of experience have demonstrated its worth, has the pattern not been widely adopted? The answer is simple. It has not been politically feasible. The majority elsewhere was dedicated to the *status quo* and had the votes to preserve it. At that moment in history radical innovation was acceptable in the Antioch community because the institution in 1920 had narrowly survived a fatal crisis. The pre-Morgan student body numbered less than sixty, the faculty only six, the total budget amounted to less than $15,000, and the buildings were in ruinous condition. Without some type of drastic action the end was near. Morgan brought in a new faculty who vastly outnumbered the surviving half dozen. These newcomers, selected for their breadth of view as well as their notable academic competence, were open to new and radical proposals. Those still alive who experienced these developments at Antioch attest that the inchoate state of affairs in 1920 and the new personnel made radical educational innovation possible. This receptiveness to new ideas which at the outset some might have considered temporary expedients was kept alive by the adversities and privations of the depression years in the thirties. Antioch was then not hobbled by the established vested interests which typically oppose any but self-serving academic reform. By the time such a restrictive group might have come into being, the radical doctrines of an earlier day had become their own traditions.

Another feature of the Antioch program provided the flexibility conducive to experimentation with new government structures. The work-study plan under which students spent a period of study on, succeeded by a period of work away from, the campus cultivated maturity of judgment and independence of action. Although Antioch did not pioneer in this venture, it was the first liberal arts college to use the plan, which it unquestionably brought to maximum effectiveness. To sustain the program required a faculty committed to innovation and experimentation, with students taking considerably more than conventional responsibility for their own education and for other decisions. Under the general conditions of life on and away from the campus, the Antioch system invalidated the *in loco parentis* doctrine, the *bête noire* of today's students. At Antioch, under the work-study plan, students were expected and urged to take responsibility for their own welfare, including participation in the formulation of educational policy.

An examination of other experimentally inclined institutions in respect to the conditions which seem to predispose them toward change is revealing. Such a review justifies the inference that substantial change occurs generally either in a crisis or with the establishment of a completely new institution. Bennington, for example, where it was possible to recruit an entirely new faculty committed to new policies and practices, has for decades maintained a policy of experimentation and full student involvement. In the older, more firmly established institutions, on the other hand, individual, departmental, or subject-matter units, and various other subculture peer groups are able either by overt action to forestall the adoption of new policies or by inanition to destroy them.

Promising innovations in higher education, the pre-war general education programs, for example, have died or continued on as breathless corpses, not because scientific evidence proved them educationally unsound, but because faculty members with a dominant position in the academic government were more concerned with the preservation of their personal and subject-matter interests.

If vested interests limit deviations in policy, the question arises as to why Antioch's radical departures adopted in crisis were not abandoned in palmier days when new faculty members arrived. The answer seems to be that prospective additions to the staff were screened in terms of their commitment to the philosophy which governed the Antioch community. Moreover, the traditions of open discussion, democratic participation, and self-determination became so well established that they themselves acquired a vested interest which the full membership of the community vigorously protected.

The reasons for the inauguration and preservation of student participation at Antioch are equally relevant answers to the question: Why have the Antioch practices, until recently, not spread more widely among other colleges and universities? Some diffusion has occurred, but until the student disturbances of recent days a mere handful of the 2,500 American institutions of higher education had even considered admitting students to faculty committees. Aside from human inertia, which in the absence of internal upheaval or external pressure generally militates against social change, the lack of student involvement can be attributed to the desire of administrators and faculty members to preserve the existing system. The common objections to giving students a part in the academic policy-making, which doubtless carry weight with the members of the establishment—student immaturity, the brevity of students' residence, their lack of knowledge, and other factors—will later be treated at length. But the primary reason for the lack of diffusion of the Antioch plan is that the constituent governing groups are satisfied with what they have and fear that their autonomy will be divided or destroyed if they share it with students.

It is crucially important that those who in hundreds of colleges and universities are grappling with the difficult problems of reconstructing academic government should recognize that the issues involved are primarily political and only secondarily educational. Whether students should be admitted to membership in academic policy-making bodies, whether they should be appointed or elected, whether they should constitute a substantial percentage of the whole membership, whether they should be allowed to vote, and many other related questions are obviously political, not educational, issues. Leaving aside the negligible group of students expressly committed to the destruction of the existing establishment, and assuming the sincerely constructive motives of the others, the primary problem then becomes one of fruitfully bringing the experience and ideas of the students into the political processes of the academic society. The crises of the past several years have given students considerable power, but the academic establishment generally has not yet found ways to harness this power to help bring about institutional improvement. Antioch and its sister institutions provide many examples to this end.

Since academic institutions apparently change only in crisis, it would seem futile to expect any widespread adoption of the Antioch plan. If only a few of the hundreds of colleges and universities have not over a half century recognized the plan's merits or considered it adaptable to their own theory or practice of government, is it realistic to expect them to do so now? For one persuasive reason, it is. The present circumstances of neither society at large nor academic life are normal. No extensive array of facts is needed to prove the present instability of social organizations, the widespread dissatisfaction, especially among youth, with the social and educational establishments, and the pervasive search for new institutional goals and new organizational forms to reach these goals. American society and American higher education are in crisis. Although the present unsettlement is not like that which begat and nourished Antioch's radical experimentation of the twenties and thirties, this study has shown unmistakably that the social fluidity of the past several years has already initiated basic changes in the patterns of academic governance. There are signs that student actions are becoming more restrained and their demands less insistent. Yet in some ways the students' efforts at reform are becoming more effective for the very reason that they are becoming more reasonable. This moment is, therefore, propitious for institutions to take fruitful advantage of the more considered student initiative.

To be sure, the Antioch plan cannot be universally adopted. Such a government structure as the administrative council, effective as it may be in a relatively small college, would not be satisfactory in a university with 40,000 students and 50 administrative units. Representation would be inadequate, the work load prohibitive, the communication system cumbersome, and to many members the subjects discussed esoteric. The essential features of the Antioch plan, and the few others roughly like it, are not, however, structural; they concern human relations. If the principle is accepted that students have a right to play a part in the determination of institutional policy, that they have a unique and valuable contribution to make in academic government, and that such participation should be an important part of their education, then even complex institutions can find the mechanisms necessary to reach these goals. Unless these propositions are accepted, the present tilting for power among the constituent academic groups will continue and the most sincere attempts at reform will abort.

Changes in Academic Government in Canada

The steps which the Canadian universities and colleges have recently taken to bring students into academic government reveal what can be accomplished rather quickly when this goal is accepted by the controlling bodies. The Canadian experience is not as old as that of Antioch, but it may be more comparable to the problems in the United States because it does embrace institutions which vary in size, purposes, sponsorship, and complexity. In fact, the developments there can shed considerable illumination on the American situation because of certain similarities in the two systems. The developments particularly in the large and distinguished universities like McGill, Toronto, and British Columbia may suggest types of governmental organization that with appropriate regard to indigenous differences could be adapted to American usage.

Events in Canada tend to support the theory, expressed earlier in connection with the reforms at Antioch and elsewhere, that major governmental reforms arise out of critical situations. Although the enterprise of higher education in Canada was not in a severe crisis five years ago, certain deeply rooted traditions were under critical reexamination first by a single individual and later by the membership of the Canadian Association of University Teachers. This professional organization, at the outset at least, was not concerned with the problem of bringing students into bodies either like the academic senate or the board of governors. Their primary objective was to assess what they considered to be a declining position of members of the teaching staff in the whole structure of academic governance.

The activities of the professors' association resulted in

joint action on the part of two organizations seriously concerned about making essential reforms while preserving the acknowledged strengths of academic government. Accordingly, the Canadian Association of University Teachers and the Association of Universities and Colleges of Canada commissioned a British educator, Sir James Duff, and an American educator, the political scientist Robert O. Berdahl, to study the governmental structures and processes of the Canadian institutions of higher education. Their report, issued in 1966, reviews the extant government patterns and recommends a number of desirable changes based upon factual evidence, practical experience, and theoretical consideration. American institutions considering alterations in their own machinery of government will find the Duff-Berdahl report a rich source of information and suggestions for changes required to bring the academic establishment into viable adjustment with the evolving social and political conditions of contemporary life.

At the outset of the Duff-Berdahl study, neither in the United States nor in Canada had the student efforts generally to gain membership in the councils of colleges and universities reached the intensity exhibited at Berkeley and Columbia. It is not surprising, therefore, that the study gives more serious attention to strengthened faculty participation in university governance than to the role of students. As can be observed in the following statement, the authors do suggest the desirability of considering the future role for students in government:

The subject of the relationship of students to university government is one which has only recently received serious consideration. But we saw enough symptoms of student dissatisfaction with their self-perceived status as "customers" of the universities to know that there will be increasing demands made in Canada for their elevation to partners (albeit unequal ones) in the "community of scholars and students." Some variations of the Berkeley disturbances may possibly occur in Canada during the coming years. The issue, then, is not whether to welcome or stifle this new wave of student sentiment, but rather how to develop channels into which it can flow constructively.[8]

The Duff-Berdahl report came out at a time when the members of the Canadian academic community had begun to accept the idea that the governmental organization required restructuring; and both faculty groups and governing bodies had already initiated discussion or action to that end. In the course of these events students intensified their agitation for representation in the reconstituted deliberative bodies.

Recognizing the impressive reforms in progress in Canada, the director of this study sought relevant information about them from the central office of the Association of Universities and Colleges in Canada and from the presidents of its constituent members. The generous response of these educators supplied a voluminous body of fact and opinion which made it possible to determine the extent and type of student involvement there, and to assess its transferability to counterparts in the United States.

A critical analysis of these materials validates the following tentative conclusions concerning the Canadian experience:

[8] *University Government in Canada,* Report of a Commission sponsored by the Canadian Association of University Teachers and the Association of Universities and Colleges of Canada (Toronto: University of Toronto Press, 1966), p. 65.

1. With few exceptions the members of the Association of Canadian Universities and Colleges have brought students into the top policy-making bodies, which until very recently included only administrative officers, faculty members, and trustees—or governors, as they are usually called. Most of the institutions which have not made such structural changes plan to do so and some have only been delayed by the necessity of legally amending their founding acts. Of the thirty institutions responding, which include virtually all the major universities, ten have admitted students to the board of governors and four others are considering doing so in an early reconstitution of these bodies. A few boards have permitted students to sit as observers without giving them legal membership. Even though several respondents declared that they had no intention of adding students either to the board or to the senate, the force of general practice throughout Canada today would suggest that in time the prevailing policy will become universal.

2. In the large majority of Canadian institutions students now generally elect or appoint their own members to sit on the senate and its committees. Since this body has broad jurisdiction over the educational program, admission and degree requirements, and the selection and retention of faculty members, students in Canada obviously enjoy an influential position far beyond that of most students in the United States. Only a few of the institutions which allow students to attend all meetings and to participate in discussions deny them the right to vote, and this atypical exclusion is in process of disappearing.

3. Canadian administrative officers overwhelmingly believe that students are making valuable contributions to the deliberations of academic bodies. Some express the view

that their experience of only several years requires caution in making predictions, but on the whole those with the longest experience consider student membership incontestably useful.

The president of the University of Victoria provides a balanced appraisal of the value of student participation, within certain carefully defined limits, which he sets forth as follows: Students should not constitute a voting majority of any university-wide committee, they should not deal with appointments and tenure, and the participants should be truly representative of student opinion. Noting these qualifications, he identifies the following real benefits:

(a) A clear understanding and appreciation of the problems of students as part of the administrative and academic process of higher education;

(b) Helpful advice from responsible students on how orderly and constructive change can occur in higher education and in the larger society;

(c) Within the accepted assumption of earlier maturing and perceptive students, better and faster insights on the purposes and methods of education.

Another judicious assessment of one university's experience with student involvement is presented by the president of the University of Windsor, who states:

We have had student membership on our Senate for the past two years, and our opinion of their performance on the Senate and in committees is highly favorable. There have been some instances where the individual students have shown insufficient interest in their duties and have not taken the necessary preparation for effective performance on specific issues. But I would have to say the same thing about some of our faculty members! In the present climate of opinion among the younger generation and university students in particular, I do believe that a sense of some participation in various academic decisions which are of keen interest to them is highly desirable. We are keenly aware of the fact that students are here today and gone tomorrow, and in that sense they have no commitment to long-range responsibility, but they have been consistently very helpful to members of the administration. I should perhaps add that we have observed in recent months that wherever there is a sense of conflict between the students and the rest of the university it has been moving away from confrontation with the administration to confrontation [with] members of the faculty . . . .

4. Not surprisingly a number of Canadian presidents expressed the view that some problems still remain to be solved. Among the most important are the proportion of students to non-students, the selection processes required to get the best-qualified representatives, the arrangements needed to assure a long enough term to maximize the students' potential contributions, a plan to free enough of the students' time to enable them to participate fully without damage to their scholastic work, and a number of like matters. No respondent suggested, however, that any problem yet visible would require reversal of the present trend toward student involvement, and some mentioned plans to enhance the student's role.

5. Lastly, the evidence suggests that it would not be extravagant to conclude that the Canadian enterprise of higher education as a whole has become committed to the doctrine that students can and should play an important role in determining the policies and practices which shape their own higher education.

The experiences of Antioch and the Canadian institutions have been treated at some length because the former shows that in at least one small institution student participation has operated successfully for a half century, and because the latter shows that student representation in academic government has been adopted and works with initial effectiveness at least, in many institutions that are much larger and have academic traditions very similar to those in the United States. Moreover, the transition from older to newer forms of government was generally accomplished, if not with complete community calm and rational discussion, at least with far less upheaval and notably less primitive behavior than in a number of American centers of learning.

The example of Canada would suggest that in principle students could be similarly enfranchised in the United States. To achieve this goal requires first the admission that conventional academic government has become inadequate to the circumstances of late-twentieth-century life. No single formula of student participation can be applied to all institutions of higher education. Since some of the unique strengths of American higher education stem from variation and autonomy, the distinctive features of the institutions ought to be preserved. But within this proper range of varied practice there is room for students to take part. And the conditions essential to governmental reform now prevail. The widespread interest among students in becoming more centrally involved in the bodies which make academic policy and the progress already made toward this end suggest a widespread acceptance of the principle of student participation. Institutions only need to find the appropriate means. Before considering means, however, it will be illuminating to review the progress already made.

A SURVEY OF EXISTING PRACTICE

No comprehensive body of fact showing the extent of student involvement in academic government has existed before, as mentioned above; accordingly, the American Academy of Arts and Sciences in late 1969 instituted this survey to determine how far the developments of student participation had proceeded. Because such a large body of detailed facts was produced, the statistics are reported in the Appendix. The main generalization which these facts permit is that although until three or four years ago American colleges and universities severely limited the involvement of students in academic government, now membership in one or another "faculty" committee is becoming the rule rather than the exception. The findings reveal that in the fall of 1969, 88.3 per cent of the 875 institutions that supplied usable information had admitted some students to membership in at least one policy-making body. It is, therefore, the atypical institution which has not moved in this direction, and such institutions are now for the most part actively considering doing so.

Those who believe that students have a right to a role in shaping educational policies will doubtless be reassured by the fact that almost nine out of ten institutions have already adopted such a policy. It would be a mistake, however, to jump from the foregoing figures to the satisfying conclusion that students are now in a position to exert strong influence on basic educational policy. Such an inference must be qualified by the facts exhibited in Table 1 (Appendix) about the kinds of committees on which students serve and their status in those bodies. No exhaustive documentation is required to demonstrate that, in terms of influence, membership in committees on social activities and entertainment, traffic and parking, homecoming, a spring festival, or a parents' day is not equivalent to voting status in the executive committee, the committee on the curriculum, on faculty selection and tenure, on admissions, or on degree requirements. Accordingly, specific information was gathered on the kinds of committees to which students had been admitted.

Students on Boards of Trustees

For some two centuries the dominant decision-making agency in the colleges and universities of the United States has been the board of trustees. Typically this board has also served as the court of last resort when the rival claims of academic groups or individuals have required adjudication at a level above the administration. Charters or acts of incorporation often spell out in detail the trustees' comprehensive legal rights and responsibilities. Even where these rights and responsibilities have not been specified, the courts have generally construed the establishing act to confer sweeping powers and obligations on the board. Board responsibilities have customarily included the establishment of institutional purposes, the exercise of fiduciary supervision over resources and properties, the determination of the general character of instructional programs, the setting of requirements for admission and graduation, and the selection of the administrative officers and members of the teaching staff.

In view of the boards' extensive powers, this study attempted to determine their policies respecting student membership. The resulting data show that students participate much less commonly in the deliberations and actions of the trustees than in those of the faculty. Although over 88 per cent of the 875 responding institutions reported some student membership in some faculty committees, the percentage reporting membership in the board of trustees shows the situation in this respect to be quite different. Only 175, or 20.0 per cent, of the institutions replying had admitted students to board meetings, and even these few were apparently unwilling to enfranchise students since only 2.7 per cent gave them voting privileges. Moreover, many presidents reported that when the board met in executive session to discuss such sensitive matters as salaries or tenure, students were asked to withdraw. In a few institutions students have recently been made regular members of important standing committees of the board of trustees with full voting power. Stanford University's trustees, for example, in September of 1969, accepting a proposal of one of its special committees, admitted students to committees on academic affairs, buildings and grounds, finance, land development, and planning and development. After consultation in accordance with established procedure, the president of the trustees may appoint two students to each of these bodies.

Perhaps the most recent and the most radical changes in academic government were voted by the board of trustees of Otterbein College on June 6, 1970. The action of this body gave students an equal and full voting voice in all phases of campus governance, on the board of trustees, and in the college senate. Three students have been added to the board along with three faculty members, and students will have an equal voice in all matters of policy including the making of the budget, the shaping of the curriculum, and the hiring of the faculty. A college senate with equal representation of students and faculty members, and presided over by the president, will determine all final policies before they go to the board for approval.

Students will be regular, full voting members of the administrative council, the budget control committee, the judicial council, the academic council, the curriculum committee, the personnel committee, campus affairs committee, campus services committee, and several others. They will elect their own representatives to all these bodies.

In terms of structure, representation, and scope of responsibility, the new government at Otterbein College is the most advanced in the entire establishment of higher education. In principle it comes closer than any other extant model to establishing a genuine academic community with all members participating in the deliberative and legislative processes which determine major educational policy. It is, of course, untried in practice, but since all persons concerned were involved in its development over a two-year period, it may reasonably be expected to function with a minimum of friction from the beginning.

Some boards seem to be willing in principle to make drastic modifications of their organic structure to accommodate students, but before initiating the necessary legal actions, which it would be awkward to rescind, they want to have definitive answers to many questions which until recently have hardly been discussed. Among others, these queries include such items as the number of students to be admitted to the board, the procedure which should be used to select them, and the length of their terms. The few institutions which have already admitted students to the board have answered some of these questions. Students have usually been selected either by direct vote of the students themselves or by virtue of holding other offices to which students have elected them. In 56 per cent of the 175 institutions, students select their representatives by election or by *ex officio* position. In only 10 of the 875 institutions did the chairman of the board or the president of the college appoint students and only one co-opted students along with other board members.

These facts about boards of trustees show that students have not generally been admitted to a board's regular sessions, but in the few institutions where this is the practice, they typically also sit with one or another of the board committees. The committees to which students have most commonly gained access are, in order of frequency: the committee on student affairs, life, or welfare; on educational policy; on the selection of the president; on buildings and grounds and the design of the campus and its structures; and on development or public relations. A few institutions also include students in over thirty other committees with different names and functions, but the representation is negligibly small. Even where students regularly attend the meetings of the board and its committees, the force of their influence remains obscure because generally they have only the privilege of discussion. The participation of students in board deliberations today unquestionably represents an advance over traditional practice, but even now membership is distinctly the exception rather than the rule.

Most colleges and universities consider the faculty executive committee or a committee with similar responsibilities the most powerful policy-making body other than the faculty as a whole. Hence the membership of students in such a body might be considered a significant measure of their involvement at the highest level of academic government. As shown in Table 1, the percentage of institutions having students on their executive committees is 22.7, something less than one in four. This proportion is not high, but whether 22.7 per cent represents an acceptable or encouraging situation must be decided in the light of the fact that until several years ago virtually no college or university had students on any major committee. The figure gains added significance in consequence of the fact that in four out of five institutions where students sit on executive committees, they also enjoy full voting privileges and, therefore, constitute a somewhat more influential voice in academic government. Yet since over three-fourths of the executive committees in colleges and universities include no students, these developments in the establishment as a whole can hardly be considered revolutionary.

The curriculum committee is another powerful body which influences policies related to the reforms which students have recently proposed. Here students' reach for influence has been more successful than in any other body, for they have achieved membership in the curriculum committee in more than half of the reporting institutions. As Table 2 (Appendix) indicates, a notably higher proportion of the smaller and less complex institutions than of the universities—typically the liberal arts colleges—have admitted students to curriculum committees. These differences may have resulted from the absence of all-embracing curricular committees in complex universities, with dozens of different types of programs leading to degrees. Information gathered separately from medical and law school deans, and casual data from graduate units, suggests that, if all the various administrative units were considered separately, the percentages for the more complex institutions would rise.

A third major committee is that with responsibility for faculty selection, promotion, and tenure. As the history of the Italian universities reveals, the right to determine membership in the guild of scholars has been jealously guarded by the profession from the beginning. Even the all-powerful student guild of Bologna could neither seize nor abridge this prerogative, and the teaching fraternity today retains much of this power. The fact that administrators and trustees may have to assume responsibility for legal commitments to prospective appointees should not obscure the real locus of power, which is in the faculty itself. What has been said about selection applies with equal force to promotion, and with even greater rigor to permanent tenure.

Under these ancient mores, the likelihood of students gaining membership in committees on faculty selection, promotion, and tenure would seem slim. Prevailing practice bears out this *a priori* inference. Of the 875 institutions, only 41, or 4.7 per cent, have admitted students to committees which select and advance members of the professional staff; and in 12 of these, students cannot vote. Without these 12 cases, student membership on faculty selection committees falls to a negligible 3.3 per cent.

As Table 1 shows, a modest percentage of institutions have also added student members to other committees rather influential in shaping educational policy and practice, such as those on planning, lectures and public events, and admissions. These developments doubtless to some extent reflect the demands students have made in some places for more liberal speakers, less rigid and more authentic requirements for admissions, and open-housing policies. In any event, such progress as has occurred still leaves students in over two-thirds of the institutions without a voice in these areas.

In sum, it would be a mistake to conclude that because students do increasingly participate in the deliberations and actions of some institutional committees, they have now gained a position of decisive or even strong influence in the bodies concerned with basic educational issues. Indeed, in spite of larger formal involvement in policy-making, the position of students in the academic community could be misconceived if social trends in the United States since World War II were not considered. The tendency of these trends, described below, has been to reduce, rather than increase, the influence of students. Each external change or marked alteration in academic life itself has minimized for many students the sense of participation in campus decisions.

One trend widely noted by everyone, and criticized by students, has been the simple increase in size of the academic enterprise. Mass life on the campus, the impersonality of the educational process, the remoteness—especially in large classes—of the instructor from the student, the lack of opportunity for out-of-class contact with teachers, the mechanization and routinization of advisory and guidance services, and the objectification and quantification of evaluation procedures have all been unfortunate concomitants of rapid growth. At the same time students complain that the substantive content of instruction has often become irrelevant to the matters which they consider of transcending importance to them as individuals and to American society as a whole. They also object to the excessive fragmentation of knowledge among departments and disciplines, the preoccupation of putative teachers with research and consultation, the involvement of academic personnel in secret and war-related research, the discrimination against the economically and educationally underprivileged, the neglect of human qualities and social virtues other than narrow and abstract intellectual competence, the accumulating evidence of the negligible relationships between academic grades and any demonstrable evidence of later success in professional life, and the narrow prescriptiveness of the curriculum.

These changes in the conditions and the ethos of academic life have been accompanied by two other adverse developments in human relationships. Since both have added to the subordination of student influence, they require careful consideration in any governmental reorganization. One is the historical fact that during the past decade students have been caught in a "sellers' market." The postwar baby boom produced a surplus of applicants for college admission at the very time when the faculty shortage was greatest, and when its members were being seduced away from their teaching obligations by the sirens of research and consultation. Under pressure, institutions concerned themselves with meeting external social and internal faculty demands instead of student needs. After analyzing reform in American colleges and universities during this period, JB Lon Hefferlin concluded that this factor accounts for much of the drop in student influence:

> ... the role of the American college student since the middle of the 1950s has become encapsulated by being rendered passive. The power—real though invisible—that students shared in earlier decades with faculty members and administrators has declined. Earlier generations of students could often set the level of classroom production required of them

by the simple device of restricting their output without threat of faculty retaliation. . . .

More recent students, however, despite appearance to the contrary, have been successively disenfranchised. With the recent surplus of applicants for admission, faculty members have been more free to raise the threat of academic failure and dismissal, and at the same time an increasing number of students have come to believe that college graduation is necessary for their personal success and have thus been reluctant to jeopardize their future by attacking the one means of this success. Thus with pressure from above to restrict the influence of students, coupled with their acquiescence in a largely impotent role, students—the largest and most immediate bloc of clients of colleges and universities—have in most institutions become encapsulated. They have proven insignificant, until the late 1960s, in effecting academic reform.[9]

Another development which has submerged students in the policy-making hierarchy is the growing acceptance among professors of the "collegial" theory of academic government. With increased power faculty members have reacted against the autocratic control of presidential leaders which dominated American colleges and universities in the nineteenth century. Patriarchal government then was, at its best, an enlightened and benevolent despotism and, at its worst, a parochial and oppressive tyranny. Now faculties are calling for a collegial style of governance in which power is dispersed among all the members of the *collegium* and where policies are determined only by the vote of its members. With this rise of faculty power and the reciprocal decline of the administrative hegemony, a patriarchal model

[9] *Dynamics of Academic Reform* (San Francisco: Jossey-Bass Inc., Publishers, 1969), p. 148.

for academic government is as outmoded as the Ptolemaic theory.

The collegial model of academic organization, which faculties favor, is a theory of government which ostensibly rests on the basic democratic principle that all who are affected by the government should have a voice in determining its policies and choosing its officers. Ideally this collegial model may indeed involve faculty members in all decision-making processes, and thus it may have considerable merit as far as it goes, but it betrays a curious blindness and inconsistency. It leaves basic institutional policy in the hands of a corpus of professionals who, like all other human beings, are largely moved by self-interest. It greatly curtails the role of boards of trustees and administrative officers, and it reduces students, the persons for whose education the collegial community supposedly exists, to customers, who merely buy what is offered. Thus the most ardent advocates of collegiality do not propose to enfranchise students along with the faculty; instead they assume students should retain their traditional role of mere clients. As the authors of *Power, Presidents, and Professors* have written:

> The students are a major clientele: they are members of a larger society who receive the benefits of the faculty's activities directly. Students are a principal "raw material" of the university: they enter the university in one state of knowledge and viewpoint and, it is hoped, leave it in another. It is the faculty, theoretically, who are mainly responsible for the transformation.[10]

[10] Nicholas J. Demerath, Richard W. Stephens, and R. Robb Taylor, *Power, Presidents, and Professors* (New York and London: Basic Books, Inc., 1967), pp. 23-24.

The last sentence in this quotation is more a dogmatic assertion or pious wish than an empirically derived principle, and the phrase "it is hoped" exhibits the patent vacuousness of most statements on the outcomes of higher education. The results of a number of careful studies—one of student values done long ago by Philip Jacobs, for example—show that subcultures on the campus other than the policy-making faculties have had greater influence on the students' total education than has formal instruction. If, as has been theoretically asserted, the faculties have been responsible for the alleged transformation in human traits, they have been notably ineffective. The collegial organization and concentration of power would, without student inclusion in the *collegium,* inevitably solidify the present unfortunate educational inadequacies and incidentally intensify students' efforts to correct them.

The whole concept of students as "raw material" to be manipulated by their all-wise professorial elders is no less repugnant to students than the earlier heavy-handed domination of a presidential patriarch was to the faculty. This "collegial" form of governance—the syndicalism of the professional—excludes the most numerous and most concerned members of the academic community from the processes of social control which most acutely affect their lives. Thus in its present form collegialism will surely not satisfy those who believe that students should play a significant role in making the policies which determine the character and quality of their education.

The current turmoil in which the nation finds itself regarding academic government and the students' role in it is not unique in the history of higher education: our present reconsideration of past practices, like earlier debates and shifts of power, is stemming from the transformation of society and the impact of these practices on academic culture. Nor are the factors contributing to this turmoil incomprehensible; the recent increases in student bodies, the decline of student influence, and the development of faculty professionalism all help explain today's agitation.

One factor, at least in its magnitude and intensity, does make the present reconsideration of the student's role particularly urgent. Today's students, having been nurtured in social activism, first in civil rights protests and then in anti-war demonstrations, have learned how effective the techniques of resistance and confrontation can be. On one campus after another they have observed that disruption, obstruction, and the resulting publicity can lead to institutional reform if petition and plea fail. Thus the traditional concept of the student as a supplicant, as an immature ward, as a mere client, cannot prevent turmoil: indeed, it will only stimulate increased resistance. Those who wish to restore to the campus the conditions indispensable to the achievement of the proper goals of an academic society, and who wish at the same time to realize the reforms necessary to correct the present shortcomings of American higher education, will earnestly consider ways to involve students in academic government. Means must be found to formalize the students' participation in the making of academic policy, to regularize their contribution, and to involve them as initiators of, rather than as the protesters against, policy.

FOR AND AGAINST STUDENT PARTICIPATION

RATIONALE FOR STUDENT PARTICIPATION

What specific reasons can be advanced for giving students a formal role in academic government? The most compelling rests on the generally accepted political proposition that in free societies all those affected by a social policy have an inalienable right to a voice in its formulation. In this sense, students are today not adequately free. Only through emancipation from the institutional restrictions imposed by others, and by full participation in academic deliberative and legislative processes, can they gain the status of self-determining individuals. Assured of these rights, they could play a not insignificant role in altering the policies and practices which they consider offensive to free men.

Institutional Professions and Actions

Students today, perhaps more clearly than any earlier generation, perceive the arresting contrasts between the demo-

cratic views of the members of the academic guild on domestic and international issues and the restricted human
relationships they condone in the society of learning. With
unprecedented awareness this generation of youth grasps
the crucial relationship between education and human
destiny. They understand that the amount and kind of
education one receives largely determines his social status,
his economic well-being, and the effectiveness of his participation in the life of his time. Aside from these private
concerns, students recognize that universal and effective
education is the *sine qua non* of our domestic well-being
and our position among the nations. Accepting this mo-
mentous view of education generally proclaimed by the
members of the academic establishment, they wonder why
the microcosm of learning should not reflect the social philosophy and political practices of the larger society of which
it is such an important part. If, as they are told, education
is of such fateful significance, and if they are to be the
recipients of its benefits, they are understandably asking
why they do not have a recognized voice in determining its
character and quality.

The Sophistication of Students Today

Another reason for students' involvement in governance
relates to the concerns and motivations of youth today.
Students' preoccupations suggest that they could be more
thoughtfully effective than their predecessors in taking part
in the reform of higher education. In contrast to earlier
generations, today's students have a more serious and informed interest in the social, economic, racial, political, and

international problems of their age. They have also become sensitively conscious of the potential therapeutic value of education in curing the ills of an ailing humanity. Unlike the teachers and parents of an earlier time, those of the seventies cannot rightly complain about the social, political, or intellectual apathy of most college and university students. In fact, the current complaint is not about lethargy, but the reverse, activism! Students are now concerned about the relationship (or the lack of it) between the exercises of the classroom, the library, and the laboratory, on the one hand, and their own existence and the conditions of life generally, on the other. Socially conscious as they now are, it is not surprising that the personal and social goals of students move them to be seriously dissatisfied with the unrepresentativeness of academic bodies and with the inadequacy of decision-making processes and the elephantine cumbersomeness of legislative action in colleges and universities. In this unprecedented intellectual concern and idealistic commitment, there is an immense potential for the thoughtful reconstruction of higher education and of American society.

Students Should Be Educated for Democratic Living

A third justification for student participation in academic government stems from ubiquitously declared goals of American institutions of higher education. Educators, particularly social philosophers, consider the preparation of youth for the exacting responsibilities of citizenship in an increasingly complex democratic society to be one of the most important purposes of colleges and universities. Yet faculty members establish, or at least unwittingly acquiesce in, practices which deny students the right to learn about, and to become skilled in the exercise of, these civic responsibilities. Examples of such contrasts in profession and practice are easy to find. Consider the selection of the outside speakers who address students in a campus lecture series. Administrators and faculty committees make prohibitive decisions without consulting, or in direct violation of, student opinion concerning the persons they wish to hear discuss the issues which they consider vital. Similarly, faculties or trustees, as in some California institutions, have abridged the students' opportunity to receive instruction from persons who are unable to meet the academic establishment's inflexible qualifying standards, but who students consider especially fitted to discuss important problems of the day. Students believe that if they had a proper role in academic government, an important dimension would be added to their education and an indispensable element to their preparation for effective citizenship.

Students Could Help Improve Higher Education

Fourth among the reasons for student participation in the deliberation of faculty bodies is that students could accelerate the correction of patent deficiencies in present curricular offerings. Even admitting the ambiguity and misunderstanding which now envelop the word "relevant," it is fair to say that many courses which students are now required to pursue do not prepare them very well to come to grips with the major problems of their personal and public lives. For a quarter of a century a small group of highly respected educators, like Robert M. Hutchins at the University of Chicago and James B. Conant at Harvard University, recognized that much college instruction merely prepares the student for further instruction and that only in the most derivative and remote sense can such teaching be considered to relate to life beyond the classroom walls. This fragmentation, specialization, and conceptualization of learning does not invalidate its usefulness for the minority of students who pursue it for vocational ends as, for example, candidates for the Ph.D. degree, but it does cause inexcusable gaps in the education of the larger majority. Since students far more than any other persons are where the educational action is —in the classroom—they are perforce better informed about educational substance and processes. The significance of higher education in the life of the average educated American would doubtless be increased if students sat on committees which determine the character and content of instruction.

Moreover, if students enjoyed membership in influential faculty committees, they might help in restoring some sense of unity and meaning to the infinitely varied course complexes which now constitute individual degree programs. The resolution of today's social, economic, racial, and philosophic issues, and the related human problems, requires that citizens have a more comprehensive knowledge and greater range of intellectual skills than undergraduate education now typically provides. The abject conditions of the poor, the hungry, the sick, and the ignorant and the means of their alleviation cannot be understood by "taking" a single course in economics, sociology, political science, or any other subject. Even when some portion of the content of such courses bears directly on the current circumstances of life, the inherent logic of a single discipline tends to limit the range of its application. Consider one example of the need for breadth of knowledge and skills in the intelligent solution of pressing problems in American culture. The social determinants of the life of the disadvantaged, and the means of their amelioration, must be approached from the position of not one or two disciplines, but from those of economics, psychology, penology, medicine, genetics, and political science, as well as other branches of learning. As students juxtapose their learning experiences in the classroom with the events in the world outside, they feel that their education is not sufficiently broad and relevant to the personal and social decisions their generation will be called upon to make if the human condition is to be improved. Rightly or wrongly, students believe that if they were given a voice in academic bodies, they could be helpful in bringing instruction closer not only to their own interests but to the conditions of modern life generally.

The Abolition of the Doctrine of In Loco Parentis

A fifth justification for student involvement concerns the general conditions, and the style, of life in the academic community. American institutions of higher education, unlike most of their European counterparts, have historically assumed the responsibility of acting on behalf of parents while their sons or daughters are in residence. Under the doctrine of *in loco parentis* institutions have regulated the lives of students and imposed the most objectionably repressive measures to govern their personal conduct. In addition to laying down scholastic regulations custodial supervision has determined the kinds of personal associations students could have, their right to leave the campus, their recreational activities, and a host of other private matters.

Many, even those who do not press for student representation in other areas of policy-making, feel that in respect to their personal lives institutions still improperly treat students like irresponsible children rather than like maturing adults. The unrealistic and futile character of this pseudoparental attitude is well illustrated in the comment of a coed in a college which includes work experience as one of the requirements for a degree. She observed that it was ridiculous to require a man to leave her dormitory room at eleven o'clock when during the previous six months she had entertained whom she pleased when she pleased and how she pleased in her South Chicago apartment. During the past several years, students have found these parietal regulations more irritating than any other rules. The choosing of human associations and the shaping of a private life, so long as these personal decisions do not restrict the freedom of others, ought to be experiences which contribute to the achievement of mature adult conduct. Since decision-making in respect to personal conduct is as essential a part of education as participation in the determination of more strictly academic policies, students can with equal propriety claim membership in academic bodies which make parietal rules.

The Improvement of Instruction

The sixth, and perhaps the most persuasive, argument for student participation in academic government rests on the special and sometimes unique information students possess about the teaching-learning situation. Students have certain experiences which qualify them to make more reliable judgments than their associates among the trustees, administrators, or faculty members. These experiences concern matters related to, but quite different from, the content of courses or the substantive relationships among them discussed earlier. Students are peculiarly situated to make judgments concerning the faculty member's performance in discharging his responsibilities in the classroom. Since custom, if not ethics, prevents all others from viewing the instructional situation, students are the only group capable of gathering the relevant facts. Only they can day by day actually observe the practitioner's fulfillment of his professional obligations—his knowledge of his subject, his preparation for the presentation of specific assignments, his attitude toward and availability to students who may need additional help, and his conscientiousness in seeing that research and consulting do not interfere with his teaching obligations.

It is generally agreed that the large increase in the number of students in recent years has interfered with the carrying out of some traditional teaching activities. That too many teachers have too many students is generally recognized, and the consequent neglect of some students under present circumstances is unavoidable. But the allowance of outside professional activities to interfere with the work of the classroom has been less widely recognized, or at least less publicized. Yet the practice of neglecting some of the traditional responsibilities of college teaching has become epidemic. Since the end of World War II it has been a problem much exacerbated by the availability to an increasing proportion of faculty members of other types of preferred professional activities—doing research, writing learned articles, and advising corporations and the government. Some members of the profession should doubtless be permitted, indeed encouraged, to devote themselves exclusively to such non-teaching responsibilities, while others give their undivided efforts to teaching. Except in such recognized cases, however, students have a right to expect presumptive teachers to teach. If students, often the sole possessors of relevant information, were given an officially recognized role in evaluating individual faculty members on established criteria of acceptable teaching performance, they might assist in the correction of the present inadequacies in teaching.

Although the case can easily be made for a role for students in the reform of teaching, it is significant that of all the policy-making bodies to which students have gained access, the committee on faculty selection, promotion, and tenure falls near the bottom of the list. Only 4.7 per cent of the 875 reporting institutions have admitted students to committees on faculty appointment, promotion, and tenure, and in only 3.3 per cent do they vote. Yet it is the faculty members who provide (or do not provide) effective instruction. When compared to the much larger percentages of membership in other committees, these figures seem to justify the inference that the profession more often favors student involvement in committees which set other policies than those which pass judgment on the effectiveness of its own membership.

Students are beginning to recognize that the character and quality of their education will be determined not so much by the kinds of persons who occupy trusteeships or administrative offices, but by the qualifications, the interests, the attitudes, and the dedication of the men and women they meet in the classroom. Moreover, they are coming to realize that the kinds of teachers they have will to a considerable extent be determined by the role students play in their selection. With students on no more than 4.7 per cent of committees on faculty selection, promotion, and tenure, their progress toward gaining this kind of influence is clearly negligible. It has often been said that the quality of education a particular institution offers is determined by the kinds of faculty members who serve it. Since students increasingly recognize this fact of academic life, and since they feel that they have constructive criticisms to make with respect to their education, they believe that they ought to have a voice in selecting staff members and evaluating their professional performance.

OBJECTIONS TO STUDENT PARTICIPATION

The foregoing arguments in favor of the involvement of students in academic government, as persuasive as they are to some, leave others unconvinced. Many informed and sincere persons firmly believe that if students gain an authentic voice in academic government, the ends of higher education will at best be confused, and at worst subverted. Their reasons for taking this position deserve thoughtful consideration.

Students Will Dominate the Academic Society

The critics' most serious question on student participation has to do with the power structure within the academic polity. The locus of power in colleges and universities is a complicated and somewhat obscure subject, which an analysis of the related legal documents is more likely to obfuscate than to illuminate. Although the cure of the maladies which now afflict the academic organism requires a discriminating diagnosis of the political forces now at work, a proper examination of this matter lies beyond the scope of the present discussion. Nevertheless, until such a review has been made, one aspect of the power structure must be given attention in any consideration of the objections to student participation.

Some opponents contend that the admission of students to important academic bodies would so alter the balance of power within them that, in fact, virtual control would shift from the board, the administration, and the faculty to the students. The antagonists to student participation do not usually spell out the theoretical results of such a realignment of control, but they do point to their concrete manifestations in some of the recent "non-negotiable" demands of activists. They show that these ultimata have included virtually the full range of institutional policies and practices. Student groups have made efforts (sometimes successfully) to eliminate individual courses and indeed whole curricula which they found objectionable and to introduce others they favored. They have caused teachers and administrators of whom for one reason or another they disapproved to be removed and other acceptable substitutes to be appointed. They have been able to halt the erection of some buildings and to initiate the construction of others. They have caused the radical revision of admission standards and the inauguration of elaborate new advisory systems. The evidence is conclusive that students have already effected many basic changes in American higher education.

And most of these results have been accomplished without official status. Witnessing all that students have achieved with the sanction of neither law nor custom, those who oppose their participation fear the more radical changes which authentic involvement might be expected to bring.

The Immaturity of Students

A second objection to student involvement concerns their youth and limited life experience. Critics consider the behavior of today's students, especially undergraduates, at times capricious and frivolous, at other times inflexible and dogmatic—in a word, immature. A judicious observer will not overlook the fact that these judgments rest largely on the behavior of students in those institutions whose turbulence has recently been the center of national attention. On these campuses many have acted with little or no regard for conventional codes of behavior. They have unconscionably violated the rights of other members of the community and capriciously established their own value system for the appraisal of human conduct. They have created their own dogmas, sometimes more unyielding than those they have been designed to replace. They have failed to display the kind of balanced judgment which is supposed to characterize the cultivated mind. In brief, however valid the students' animadversions against the academic establishment may be, critics believe that youth's efforts at reform have often lacked the intellectual and emotional restraint associated with maturity. Defenders of students say that this is too much to expect from young people in their late teens or early twenties. The opposition promptly agrees with this judgment and cites it as their primary reason for not giving students a decisive role in academic government.

The Brief Involvement of Students

In the matter of student participation the members of the profession voice a third reservation. They point out that most students, especially the numerous undergraduates, spend only four years in any one institution, and many spend only a year or two. Under these circumstances some of the more permanent staff members question whether even the most earnest students can acquire the perspective and the commitment essential to sound judgment on long-term policies. These senior professionals doubt not only that students can deal prudently with the issues and problems related to the destiny of a college or university, but that they can deal wisely with the personal well-being of the large company who have cast their lot with it. A typically brief association, it is contended, will predispose students to be interested primarily in policies of immediate benefit to themselves.

Critics cite an increase in tuition fees as an example of conflict between immediate personal and more permanent institutional values. To prevent a rise in the cost of their education, students have demonstrated against the imposition of higher fees. Yet a balanced concern for the long-term quality of the faculty and the general maintenance of standards might at a particular time require acceptance of such an action. Similarly, the adoption of fashionable but exotic curricular proposals may satisfy the passing fancy of short-term residents, but may not be in the best interest of institutional stability and economic soundness. The critics buttress their view by pointing out that students' indifference to long-run institutional welfare is confirmed by the shallow and transient concern of alumni, whose devotion to alma mater, once they have gained the degree, rapidly evaporates. Many faculty members, some of whom give a whole professional life to a particular institution, contend that neither their own nor the institution's welfare should be placed in the hands of those with such ephemeral commitments. That this view does not spring from a prejudice against students is proven by the fact that it has been applied to young faculty members in the lower ranks, who, because of their probable short service, are denied faculty status. The argument based on the shortness of institutional affiliation is one which advocates of student participation have yet to deal with adequately.

Ignorance of Professional Values

A fourth objection to a larger role for students in academic government is related to, but differs basically from, the shortness of the students' institutional affiliation. It is also related to maturity but specifically concerns one of its components, specialized abilities, and embraces the rich complement of comprehensive knowledge and special skills that is involved in the broad practice of a profession. The components of understanding, esoteric knowledge, and seasoned judgment that characterize the expert and confident practitioner of any profession are acquired slowly. Yet, to an extraordinary degree, those who have risen to the highest pinnacle of professional success have exhibited these essential and unique qualities. One need only mention such names as Charles W. Eliot, William James, Sir William Osler, and Joseph Storey to prove the point that genuine professionalism comprises not only a complex of specialized knowledge and skill, but a keen awareness of the meaning of a calling in relation to the larger human enterprise.

Now, to be sure, not all members of a profession such as teaching, even those with senior status, achieve the fullness of knowledge and the ripeness of judgment characteristic of its examplars. All do, however, grow in these respects as they practice their craft. This is especially true of college and university faculty members whose profession not only permits, but requires, the evaluation of prospective policies within a larger social context. If the forward motion of the academic enterprise is slow, it is in part because its members are sensitive to the values they have a moral responsibility to protect and preserve. Knowing as they do how priceless and yet how tenuous are the privileges of academic life, faculty members are loath to share responsibility for their preservation with the uninitiated. They object, therefore, to enfranchising students in regard to matters with which they can at best be uninformedly sympathetic and at worst callously indifferent.

Interference with Study and Gainful Employment

A fifth objection to student participation comes from some educators who oppose it not in principle, but for the practical reason that in the nature of things students cannot give the time necessary for a faithful discharge of their responsibilities. Those critics who have had the experience of meeting with committees for several hours a week sometimes for a full academic year or more know what a distractive burden such activities can be. They doubt whether even the ablest student could devote the required large proportion of his out-of-class time to committee work without adversely affecting his educational progress. The experience of entirely sympathetic academic administrators here and in Canada where students have sat on faculty committees supports this *a priori* conclusion. Some students have offered similar testimony either by direct statement or by their increasing absence from meetings as the growing burden of work has interfered with their academic obligations. Moreover, as students realize the weight of the responsibilities imposed by their obligation to report what has transpired in committee to their constituency, the whole student body, and to seek a consensus on at least the most important issues under discussion, they find themselves in a serious moral conflict. They have to choose whether they will neglect their studies at great personal sacrifice or neglect their representational obligations at the expense of their fellow students. Many unbiased persons believe that until some way is found out of this dilemma, it is delusive and futile to advocate or accept student representation in academic policy-making bodies.

SUMMARY

An evaluation of the arguments advanced for and against student participation in academic government permits the drawing of some practically useful, if not definitive, conclusions. In this unsettled stage in the evolution of new mechanisms for academic decision-making, no one can be dogmatic or authoritative about which policies will finally turn out to be unassailably sound, and which impracticable. In addition to those involving students, various other experiments are now being tried in academic government. They include innovations relating to the composition, structure, and functions of boards of trustees; the relationships between the board, the administration, and the faculty; the functions of the central administration and the departmental heads; and beyond these internal groups, the political relationships with the sustaining constituencies whether they be taxpayers or private donors. These and other matters relevant to any full treatment of academic government lie outside the scope of this paper. Even if these factors had been included, the fact that they are all in a state of flux may in time result in their having a quite different bearing on student participation than they do at present.

Nevertheless, the available body of fact and informed opinion does suggest some potentially useful conclusions about the merits of student participation and the conditions under which it would most likely benefit the establishment of higher learning and more importantly enhance the education of its patrons.

1. The weight of opinion and practice indicates wide acceptance of the idea that students should have some voice in the bodies which determine the purposes and the programs of institutions of higher education. Since virtually every committee to one degree or another deals with matters which affect the character and the quality of the students' education, and since students' experience may often shed peculiar light on these matters, it is reasonable that students should hold membership in *all* such deliberative bodies. Since, however, the interests and potential contribution of

students would inevitably vary in accordance with the differences in specific responsibilities between one committee and another, the proportion of student representation should doubtless also vary.

2. Except those on the radical fringe, almost no members of the academic society contend that because students are the most numerous citizens of the commonwealth of learning, they should uniformly have majority representation in its deliberative bodies. On the other hand, the idea advanced by the most adamant representatives of vested scholastic interests that student involvement eventually means complete confiscation of political power is no more than a red herring. Canadian institutions with substantial if brief experience with student involvement, as well as the few in the United States with traditional participation, testify that after a brief period of adjustment to their newfound power, students generally behave with customary academic decorum and consideration for their associates; and even where they consider their representation disproportionately small, they do not demand numerical dominance.

On one aspect of the balance of power between students and faculty members and the administration, experience sheds particular light. The assumption that continuing conflicts of interest among these groups will cause a constant splitting of the vote along party lines is denied by the facts. Where students have been admitted to faculty committees, they have not precipitated a partisan polarization of views. Students and faculty members rarely line up in opposing camps, even though at times selfish interest would move them to do so. At Antioch, for example, there have been only two instances in years in which the students and the faculty members on the administrative council have been irreconcilably divided.

Anyone who has had experience with the indissoluble factional differences among the members of faculty committees would not consider the danger of polarization a defensible argument against student participation. Where faculty and student groups have deliberated together, differences of opinion have usually been resolved through discussion and the results have led to a consensus acceptable to the larger constituency. To be sure, some institutions, in view of their traditions, could *ab initio* not achieve democratic working relationships. But there is no apparent reason to assume that running feuds between students and non-students would result from a mixed membership in academic bodies.

3. In maturity of conduct and judgment, students seem to vary with their experience and their length of service in deliberative bodies. The responses from presidents here and in Canada indicate that in their first meetings some students tended to be defensively aggressive and needlessly talkative. On the positive side, faculty members and administrators with experience reported that students do introduce into committee discussions points of view and facts which other participants may not be in a position to have. To this extent students enrich the policy-making process and make the outcome more acceptable to those who have to live under it.

In summary, the facts permit the generalization that the institutions having the longest experience with an academic government involving students feel that on balance it has real advantages over governmental structures dominated by an administrative patriarchy or a faculty oligarchy. Any government, of course, which assures all its constituents the rights of free speech and the ballot will suffer strains, conflict, and occasionally vigorous reaction to majority opinion. Institutions which have had student participation for years have experienced these inevitable accompaniments of democratic living. There is no widespread feeling among their members, however, that under more conventional forms of government their parliamentary difficulties would have been eased, the interests of constituent groups more fairly represented, or their business more efficiently conducted.

This generalization must be qualified with the observation that those institutions which have had the longest and most successful record of student participation inaugurated it when life in the United States at large and on the campus in particular differed markedly from the conditions which prevail today. These changed circumstances do not necessarily argue against student involvement. On the contrary, they suggest the very reverse; that is, greater student participation may be required to solve some of the current problems involved in adjusting higher education to the social conditions of life in the seventies. But the needed changes will probably be more smoothly accomplished if the altered context of reform is understood.

This presentation of the arguments for and against student participation has proceeded from the basic conviction that the student's own future well-being and the quality and condition of our national life will be largely determined by the kind of higher education he and his successors receive. It stands on the principle, therefore, that the student and the whole society have a fateful stake in the character and quality of higher education. Consequently, it supports the view that students have a clear right to a formalized voice in the establishment of the purposes and in the shaping of the policies and practices of colleges and universities. It rejects the hypothesis that students are intellectually, emotionally, and socially too immature to evaluate the educational programs and the other features of institutional life which so profoundly affect their personal welfare and happiness. It questions how students whom faculty members consider sufficiently mature intellectually and morally to study understandingly such works as Plato's *Republic,* Aristotle's *Politics,* Aquinas' *Summa Theologica,* Kant's *Critique of Pure Reason,* Shakespeare's *Hamlet* and *Macbeth,* Whitehead and Russell's *Principia Mathematica,* Freud's *Introduction to Psychoanalysis,* Wundt's *Volkerpsychologie,* to say nothing of the demanding treatises in modern physics, can challenge their ability to comprehend and deal with the theoretical issues and the practical problems of the academic establishment.

This presentation advances the case for student participation on the basic principle that undergirds any free social order: that citizens generally ought to have a voice in, and are capable of, determining the character of the social institutions which in turn determine the character and quality of their own lives. A large percentage of students today believe that they do not have such a voice. At the same time they consider theoretically invalid and pragmatically unsound some of the prevailing academic policies and practices. Thoughtful observers of the present breakdown in the traditional conditions in academic life differ in their ideas concerning what reforms are needed and how they are to be accomplished. But they exhibit a considerable consensus that students must play an influential role in the revisions of these policies and practices. Hence the circumstances of life in institutions of higher education reveal that the issue whether students should be involved in governance is now academic. The question is not *whether* students should participate, but how, to what extent, and through what innovations in organization and procedure this involvement can be most expeditiously and effectively achieved.

TECHNIQUES FOR ACHIEVING STUDENT PARTICIPATION

Abolition of the Term "Student Government"

Any consideration of the mechanisms required to bring students appropriately into the structures and processes of academic government can be simplified by disposing at the outset of the anachronistic and misleading locution "student government." Earlier, it was shown that in the past century some students in some American colleges and universities significantly influenced educational policies and practices. It would be historically inaccurate, however, to infer that these accomplishments were effected through the efforts of the various organizations known as "student government." The self-determination students enjoyed under this type of organization related to their social rather than their scholastic lives, and even in the former sphere their actions were limited. Whatever the earlier usefulness of the term, students of the 1970's find the older connotation of "student government" completely inconsistent with their own conception of their role in the government of the modern college or university. For several reasons the term ought to be abandoned.

72

First, it rests on the footless assumption and belittling insinuation that the students' activities outside the classroom, laboratory, or library have no educational significance and can, therefore, be placed in their own hands. In the light of the findings of modern psychology and philosophy—any view that learning, yes, even the most important learning—takes place only in formal instruction is patently untenable. Regrettably, many faculty members seem to embrace this philosophy in practice if not in theory. It permits them to intellectualize still further the already too detached and devitalized exercises of the classroom, and it relieves them of responsibility for any aspect of the student's life other than the acquisition of their own particular range of specialized knowledge. Not surprisingly, students are in revolt against this artificial separation of human traits and functions. Their concept of the wholeness of man and their demand for the humanization of the institutional experience are in direct conflict with a division of responsibility for various aspects of higher education between students and members of the profession.

Second, the allocation under "student government" of responsibility for different types of learning activities violates the whole concept of community. The advocates of student participation rest their case largely on the concept that all members of the academic society have a right to share in the making of the rules and laws under which they are governed. Hence it follows that students and faculty members ought to act jointly in their efforts to formulate the policies under which all will live. If student government has any future, it would seem to lie in a merger with the activities of faculty committees. In any event, the term "student government" ought to be dropped because it does not fit the circumstances of modern academic life.

PRACTICAL PROBLEMS OF STUDENT PARTICIPATION

Even after an institution decides that students have a legitimate role to play in bodies which establish academic policy, several practical problems remain to be solved, such as what proportion of the total membership students should be, by what method they should be selected, and whether they should have the right to full voting privileges.

Proportion of Student Membership

The study on which this paper is based reveals that institutions vary conspicuously in respect to the number of students they seat on faculty committees. In some the proportion rises to a third or more, but in the 875 institutions considered, many of the committees which number a dozen or more members include only one or two students. This limited membership is at best mere tokenism and at worst disingenuous power politics. The question of numbers must finally be answered in terms of fairness and equity to all members of the academic society. The rapidly changing conditions of human relationships in these communities make most serious students of academic government reluctant to express firm opinions on this subject.

An occasional proponent of student representation argues that in a completely democratic academic society in which all electors are presumptively equally qualified to cast their ballots, the Supreme Court doctrine of one man, one vote can be the only applicable principle. Applied to the academy this opinion claims too much. Special conditions prevail in the community of learning which make the doctrine of one man, one vote as unfair to some as complete disenfranchisement is now to others. In theory, application of this rule to the selection of the members of all academic legislative bodies would transfer power completely from the board, the administration, and the faculty to the students, and in most institutions, because of their numbers, to the undergraduates. Only the most incontinent advocates of governmental reform urge such a radical reconstruction. Indeed, most institutions could not inaugurate such basic transfers of legislative responsibility without a statutory or executive revision of the legal documents under which they were created and now conduct their business. In the matter of proportionate representation academic societies are not, and cannot be, completely democratic organizations. All their members—the trustees, the faculty, the administrators, the students, and the subject-matter departments—belong to subcultures with unequatable interests, knowledge, and expertise.

Aside from their numerical size, these groups differ in a significant respect—the duration of their association with an institution. Many trustees and faculty members serve a college or university for most of their adult years. Students, on the other hand, typically reside in one academic community no longer than four years and many leave at the end of one or two.

The weight of theoretical opinion, which favors a substantial majority of non-students in academic bodies, is supported by practical considerations. An institution of learning must be sufficiently stable to enable those who are teaching and learning, those who are doing research, those who are writing learned treatises, and those who are giving their time and efforts as trustees to carry on their activities with a minimum of vacillation in policy and disruption in practice. To perform their services effectively, colleges and universities must have, and be able to publicize, a reasonably enduring set of purposes, programs, faculty complement, and general living conditions. Anyone who understands the essential nature and the peculiar functions of the enterprise of higher education expects this type of stability. The members of the various groups which make up a society of learning tend to be attracted to an institution which can assure them at least the minimum of steadiness required for satisfactory working and living conditions.

Consider first those who have legal responsibility for the preservation, protection, and advancement of an academic institution—the trustees. These men and women generally have so imposing a social position and such public stature that institutions compete for their services. On the other hand, the leaders in industry, commerce, and government from among whom trustees are typically drawn carry heavy responsibilities. They understandably hesitate to give their time and energy to institutions about whose future no reliable predictions can be made. In the main the most desirable trustees will serve only institutions which show sufficient continuity of policy and personnel to guarantee that their efforts will be personally satisfying, institutionally beneficial, and socially productive.

Another group, prospective benefactors, on whom over a thousand American institutions of higher learning depend for the bulk of their external support, investigate with increasing care the internal condition and the probable future health of the intended objects of their philanthropy. They do not object to, and in fact the more discriminating donors increasingly look for, the vital institution which will use their gifts to support promising innovation and experimentation. But they will not contribute to institutions whose constantly shifting policies and personnel suggest an unpredictable future.

Third, many able men have recently left administrative posts because of the frustrating, debilitating, and vaguely defined responsibilities which these positions involved. In recent years an aggregate of several hundred presidencies have been vacant at any particular time, and the unfilled lower administrative offices have normally been more numerous. Whether these posts can be filled with men and women of acknowledged professional success or promise remains to be seen. Certain it is that the present competition will make it more difficult for institutions with records of vacillating policies and rapidly changing personnel to attract the best-qualified leaders. Men and women of real stature will not risk their professional future on the possibly capricious actions of rapidly changing and ill-informed academic bodies.

Fourth, more than at any time in the history of American higher education until very recently, the most highly qualified faculty members have been free to choose their place of employment. Among other things, the growing production of Ph.D.'s may correspondingly reduce the freedom to move, at least in the lower ranks. For some years yet to come, however, the best-qualified senior members will be in constant demand. Other things being equal, they will choose a professional affiliation which offers stable working and living conditions. They will also seek institutions where their voice will be heard in the legislative bodies which determine their professional activities and the general conditions of community life. Before accepting an appointment they will want some assurance that the major purposes and programs of the institution of their choice will not fluctuate with the fitful impulses or the shifting membership of policy-making bodies.

Lastly, prospective students themselves critically examine the educational program and the academic ethos in the institution where they may spend four years. It would be an exaggeration to say that any substantial number of high school students would *choose* a college or university because it assured them full participation in policy-making. Most prospective freshmen are not that knowledgeable about the politics of academic life. Many students will, however, decide to *remain* in an institution on the basis of their feeling that they play or do not play a role in decision-making.

Thus, all groups within the society of learning, and many outside supporters as well, have a clear interest in the maintenance of institutional stability. Ideally, any body which establishes major policies ought to have a sufficiently changing membership to assure the infusion of new ideas, balanced with a sufficiently continuing membership to assure the steadiness essential to the achievement of its purposes. There is then no single conclusive response to the question, "What proportion of the members of academic bodies should be students?" The only practically useful answer now seems to be that the membership should include students and non-students, the numbers of each varying with the types of issues which come before a particular committee and with the special knowledge and expertise required for their solution. It does seem reasonable, however, that the very decision with respect to proportionate membership itself should be reached through joint consid-eration by representatives of the constituent groups.

The background of experience. As important as continuing association may be, it should not be the dominant factor in determining the balance between students and non-students. A more compelling consideration should be the knowledge and the experience which various persons can bring to the discussions of academic issues.

Method of Selection of Student Representatives

Even if the other two dominant groups in the academic community, the trustees and the faculty, reach a consensus that students should hold membership in policy-making bodies, a critical problem will remain—that of determining the method of their selection. The facts in this inquiry clearly indicate that at present students themselves pre-ponderantly choose their representatives. In over 50 per cent of the institutions studied, student representatives are either chosen by students, or they hold membership by virtue of the offices to which they have been elected by students, or they are appointed by administrators from panels submitted by students. In less than one in ten of the institutions with students on committees are the students appointed by the president or another administrative officer. The remaining percentage involves a variety of combined methods of selection involving students, faculty members, and administrative officers. Not surprisingly, conversations with students revealed that they have little confidence in the students appointed by administrators, or in fact in any means of selection other than their own unrestricted vote. The prevailing opinion seems to be that anyone who truly believes that the voice of students ought to be heard in academic councils can hardly object if they claim the right to choose their own spokesmen.

Student rejection of elected representatives. One of the most nettling problems in constituting an academic body with student representation is created by students themselves. In the matter of determining who their spokesmen should be, a not insignificant group of the more radical exponents of government reorganization looks with disfavor on any system under which student representatives are to be chosen in an open, unrestricted, general election. These critics of the normal democratic process of selecting representatives believe that the majority of students have been so conditioned ideologically by the establishmentarian views of their elders and contemporaries that they have *ipso facto* disqualified themselves as representatives of minority political opinions. Students elected by a majority vote, they feel, would of necessity be unalterably committed to the repugnant ideas which the more radical consider responsible for most of our current social and educational ills.

Hence a deep-seated conflict exists on campuses today between a minority which, frustrated by earlier failures to achieve reform, now feels it necessary to replace reason and persuasion with unreason and coercion, and the majority, which believes that the necessary changes can still be accomplished through a restructured government in which parliamentary debate and majority decision will prevail. Even though the latter are disenchanted with many characteristics of higher education today, and the processes by which it is shaped, they feel nevertheless that in the long run the only satisfactory way out of their present dilemma is still through rational discussion, freedom of speech, and unrestricted political action. Even though recognizing that the democratic process is not a perfect device for achieving human progress, these students believe that they can gain the desired reforms in education and in society at large only through the continued selection of their representatives by free elections. They believe that to permit splinter groups of either the radical left or right *per se* to choose their own partisan representatives on academic bodies would violate the basic principles and practices of a free society. Moreover, as has already been made evident on some campuses, this plan is totally unworkable because emerging ideological differences have already caused splinter groups to splinter. The abandonment of the principle of general representation then makes impossible any consensus on major issues and leads to a paralysis of government. On some campuses this unfortunate development has gone so far that agreement cannot even be reached on the methods to be used in arriving at a generally acceptable set of parliamentary procedures to guarantee the orderly conduct of business, to say nothing of dealing with the important substantive matters that demand consideration. The next step in this deterioration of the democratic process is dictatorship.

Voting Rights for Students

In respect to the students' right to vote, current practices leave much to be desired. Of the 199 institutions where students sat with the executive committee, 33 did not allow them to vote. The corresponding figures for curriculum committees were 506 and 78; and for the committee on faculty selection, promotion, and tenure, the figure for student membership was a mere 41, with 10 not voting. Without the right to vote, even the modest present representation obviously exaggerates the students' actual influence on policy. It is a fair assumption that this exclusion creates a sense of privation and alienation, a feeling among the students that they are really not full-fledged members of the academic community. If students are to sit as authentic members of faculty and board committees, they ought to have the same voting rights as all others. This arrangement does not preclude committees from inviting other students to participate in their deliberations *ad interim* without vote as the subject under discussion and their own special competence suggest.

Proportionate representation. The decision to grant students full voting privileges immediately raises again the thorny issue of the proper proportion of their representation in relation to non-students. Even faculty members and administrators who contend that non-students should constitute a majority in all major policy-making bodies would probably agree that typically the present percentage of students is inexcusably small. In view of what they have at stake, and their special knowledge in regard to certain issues, it would not seem unreasonable to raise the student proportion in most committees to as much as a third or two-fifths. A contingent of such size would increase the latent influence of their vote and simultaneously enhance their feeling of genuine participation.

Those who fear that a substantial or even predominant

membership would enable students to take over the apparatus of government should be reassured by experience in other institutions. As already shown, experience explodes the assumption of a probable division of votes with students and non-students inevitably opposing one another. Such a discrete polarization may have been natural under an earlier form of patriarchal government, and the collegial arrangement under which the faculty dominates the decision-making process will doubtless foster partisan separatism. Experience suggests, however, that a genuine community type of academic organization will encourage students, as well as others, to put the common good above their own group interests. Here again, the Antioch experience bears convincing testimony. For decades the administrative council, the dominant policy-making body, has been composed of students, faculty members, and administrators. Yet on any significant issue a clean division of students and non-students has rarely occurred. If institutions precipitately adopted the democratic traditions of Antioch, which have a pattern of patriarchal or collegial government reaching back almost fifty years, the results might, at least temporarily, be less satisfactory. Yet Antioch has demonstrated that when students enjoy the rights and responsibilities of citizenship in a free social order, they almost uniformly discharge their obligations thoughtfully, diligently, and with an arresting dedication to public rather than personal ends. More recently other colleges and universities have also learned that when students are treated with respect and understanding, they usually respond in kind.

RESTRUCTURING ACADEMIC GOVERNMENT

The Academic Society, Community of Learning

The cause of much of the recent widespread misunderstanding between students and academic personnel arises out of the false fear among the latter that as a group, students will in principle oppose any point of view or course of action advanced by the other members of the academic community. This view reflects the pernicious conception that the academic society—which in the best sense should be a community of learning—must be composed of subgroups whose interests by the nature of things are competitive. The running feud between faculties and administrators confirms this version of class conflict, and the shifting of power in recent years tends to validate this view of partisan academic politics. The faculty as a whole acquired political strength *vis-à-vis* the administration and the trustees. Further, the constituent departmental units have established vested interests of their own *vis-à-vis* the faculty and gained the power to preserve and enhance them. These unhealthful developments, with their attendant grasp for self-serving political power, deserve to be reviewed while the role of students is under consideration. No system of government founded on the principle that its chief function is to adjudicate the differences among competing peer cultures can either restore order in the house of learning or cope with the urgent social needs of the late twentieth century.

In one of the most perceptive current analyses of academic society, a group of faculty members and students at Berkeley has exposed the anachronistic character of this view. As they see it:

Clearly the campus "society" is here viewed as a collection of status-bound interest groups, each having a special preserve and each possessing claims to participation in varying degrees—subject to negotiation—in the activities assigned to the other components. The political problem set by this approach is one of devising institutions and procedures that will enable each group to pursue its particular concerns as efficiently and harmoniously as possible in areas that overlap with those of the other groups. Politics, in this view, consists of finding techniques for promoting particular interests and conciliating conflicting ones.

Although this view may be an accurate description of our present situation, we do not regard it as an adequate, much less ideal, process for creating an educational setting fit for the cultivation of the mind and the strengthening of the human spirit. Most issues of university policy are questions requiring qualitative judgments rooted in values and principles. Such questions cannot readily be broken down into component units over which highly politicized interest groups can bargain and for which some mutually agreeable form of distributive justice can be arranged. Moreover, an issue of university principle should not be decided on the basis of which group has the most bargaining power. To pursue university policy as a task of trading off the interests of competing groups is especially damaging because the interests themselves often remain unexamined and no process exists by which the community as a whole can openly assess the cumulative effect of many isolated exchanges on the value and direction of the institution. Hence, a major weakness of the interest group conception of university policy-making has been that it has imposed narrow and artificial limits on the process of discussion and decision in the university. Moreover, it has obscured the special character of a university by regarding it much as one does any other pluralistic society populated by diverse interest groups and lacking a common commitment to anything more than the bargaining process itself.[11]

[11] Caleb Foote, Henry Mayer, and associates, *The Culture of the University: Governance and Education* (San Francisco: Jossey-Bass, Inc., Publishers, 1968), pp. 17-18.

Two recent proposals for academic reorganization seem on the surface to be calculated to bring students into the policy-making process, but at basis they are really in conflict with the foregoing view. They deserve special consideration because they seem to give students a larger role but, in fact, fall far short in very significant psychological respects. In the broad they fail to establish an atmosphere of community, and in particular they perpetuate the students' feeling that their opinions are solicited *ex post facto:* that is, after faculties and boards have already discussed and established new policies.

The "Accountability" Theory

The first plan proposed for reorganization of academic government retains the concentration of power characteristic of the patriarchal type of organization. Through the delegation of responsibility by the trustees and the faculty, the president enjoys considerable discretion in the exercise of administrative leadership. At the pleasure of the board he holds office for a specified term, during which he may initiate, and sometimes unilaterally make, such changes in policy as commend themselves. The advocates of this type of organization consider its basic principle to be "accountability." That is to say, after a period of service during which the president enjoys a considerable independence, he gives an accounting of his administration and submits to an official review of his activities by his associates—faculty members and students. Since this plan involves less prior consideration of policy with various deliberative bodies, it may result in more expeditious handling of academic business and an economy of time and effort. Because of its singleness of purpose, it may also effect a more efficient execution of a comprehensive plan of institutional development. In years past some of the most celebrated American institutions of higher education, such as Harvard, Johns Hopkins, and Chicago, achieved their distinction under this type of governmental organization and single-minded leadership.

There are, however, at least three major weaknesses in the accountability theory. The first relates to the scope and the detail of the accounting the administrator can be expected to make to the other members of the community. Unless actions for which officials are to be accountable are spelled out in detail, incumbents tend to account only for such of their decisions and actions as they consider appropriate. Myriad cases of administrative misconduct brought before the American Association of University Professors reveal wide differences of opinion between faculty members and administrators concerning the scope of administrative answerability. The group relationships that have hitherto prevailed on campuses would indicate that the higher echelons of administrative officers, and faculty members as well, have been more inclined to report on than to account for their actions. The doctrine of accountability would probably work well only with personalities who as a matter of course operate on the democratic basis of currently seeking advice and criticism.

A more significant weakness in the accountability theory arises out of the conception of the academic society on which it rests. It presupposes an academic hierarchy which faculty members have challenged for years, and it involves a pattern of human relationships which students today reject out of hand. "Accountability" is basically incompatible with the idea of a community of persons with diverse individual interests but united by adherence to a set of common goals and commitments. It enables an executive who wishes to do so temporarily at least to disregard the claims of students and others to the right to a voice in making the policies which govern them. Some of the most vexatious disturbances of recent days have arisen not so much from an out-and-out refusal of institutional officers to accede to specific student demands, but rather from their unwillingness to accept the basic principle that students have a legitimate role to play *from the very beginning* in all deliberations on matters of common concern. Accounting for decisions after the fact obviously violates the spirit if not the letter of a democratic academic government.

These two procedural defects in the "accountability plan" are accompanied by a third substantive weakness. Experience has shown that serious students have significant and sometimes unique contributions to make to academic discussions. If these views have potential value, they should be introduced into the initial discussions of policies, not added as commentaries of dissent or approval on decisions already taken.

Aside from the psychological objections to such a peripheral involvement, accountability has the practical disadvantage of postponing the resolution of problems which prior consultation might have forestalled. In the scholastic ethos of the 1970's *ex post facto* referrals are likely to be less fruitful and acceptable than authentic participation in the original formulation of policy. If accountability means periodic reporting by administrative officers to various constituencies, then both students and faculty members will not find it acceptable because it leaves them substantially where they have been in academic government, that is, outside its main structure and processes. Another type of accountability might be less objectionable. Under this plan, before taking any action, responsible officers would refer proposed actions to the appropriate constituent bodies with their recommendations and a request for approval or modifications. They would also continuously solicit proposals for changes in policy. But this arrangement would not conform to the currently proposed theory of accountability because it substitutes ongoing involvement of the whole community for periodic reporting.

A Modified Tripartite Form of Government

The second proposal for academic government would preserve many features of the present governmental structure with its tripartite division of responsibilities among the trustees, administrative officers, and faculty members. The trustees would retain *legal* policy-making powers over all aspects of institutional life, but they would continue to delegate to the faculty and administrative officers extensive control over the educational program and day-by-day operations. Under this arrangement the faculty would be a separate legislative body with dominant power over educational policy, for example, requirements for admission and degrees, curricular content, and parietal rules.

A fourth and largest group in the academic community, and the chief reason for its being, the students, would be added but would as at present have little authentic voice in institutional policy-making. The proponents of a government organization with four separate units acknowledge that both historically and currently students have occupied a weak and obscure position in the power structure, and they generally favor giving students a larger voice in legislative action. Instead of joining all four groups in a common body, however, and thus raising students to a comparable position in the company of faculty members, administrators, and trustees, they would allocate to students jurisdiction over institutional matters of peculiar concern to them, to be handled in an organization of their own. The actions resulting from student deliberations would then be brought before corresponding bodies of the faculty and the board for their review and action. As in present practice, the major policies of the faculty would be reviewed and acted upon by the trustees.

This type of organization rests on the principle that each of the constituent groups in the academic society has separable interests of its own, with which, in the first instance at least, the several constituent groups can deal more effectively individually than collectively. The final resolution of differences would either be achieved as at present by the action of the successive groups in the hierarchy or through the creation of some sort of superbody including representatives of all groups. Like the accountability theory of government, this arrangement has obvious advantages. It particularizes and limits the matters to be considered by each legislative body. Except to rubber-stamp them, trustees need not concern themselves with such matters as new programs of study; faculty members need not be concerned about the erection of buildings; students need not consider these or a host of other matters traditionally reserved to the faculty and to the trustees. Students would, to be sure, have responsibility for making certain types of policy, but these would generally be limited to problems of their social life which for decades have been handled by student government. Eventually all matters of major and general concern which transcended the spheres of group interests would be brought before a more representative governmental agency for approval, rejection, or continuing study.

Whatever its merits, this structure preserves some of the features of government to which both faculty and students now object. It minimizes the opportunity for common consideration of common problems. It fails to provide for continuous intercommunication among groups in the academic society who may have different views on issues, the resolution of which affect all. It permits and in some instances encourages the hardening of unacceptable positions within the three constituent groups, and consequently prolongs discussion of problems that might have been amicably resolved with a free exchange of views early on. Matters which through unilateral action would have become "nonnegotiable" doubtless in many cases remain subject to normal parliamentary disposal. Most importantly, such a structure nullifies the one feature of government most likely today to restore amity in academic society—a genuine sense of community. If this feeling of involvement, the sense that the academic citizen has not only a stake but an inescapable responsibility in government, could be inculcated in all, it might be the factor that could result in a unification of effort toward generally acceptable goals. It could also reduce to a human minimum the political maneuvering for the preservation of vested party interests which now so often divides the member groups in the academic commonwealth. Whatever its merits in delimiting powers and clarifying issues within the members of the constituent groups, a tripartite —or quadripartite—form of government does not appear to be acceptable today as a device that would at once resolve current political conflicts and assure the considered treatment of the issues which now afflict the house of learning.

The Advancement of Education

An entirely different conception of the academic community and of the values which invest its purposes and activities is required in any defensible reorganization of its government. The basic plank in the new academic political platform ought to be the idea that the dominant mission of the institution is the advancement of education, not the enhancement and strengthening of party groups. And the word "education" requires broad definition. It must include every influence and condition of living in the academic community which shapes the lives of those who come there to be educated. A definition may begin with the substantive material transmitted in the classroom, the seminar, the library, and the laboratory. It may also emphasize the didactic processes by which formal knowledge passes from the teacher to the student. But in terms of the findings of modern psychology relating to the educational impact of the whole environment and the indispensable value of the students' full intellectual and emotional involvement in the learning process, such a narrow conception of higher education is indefensible. Every force in the community which shapes the mind and character of the student must be considered educational. The broadest but not necessarily a numerically equal representation of all its members will assure the fullest consideration of the issues involved. In this process students have a contribution to make to the discussions of educational theory and practice.

The ends of education and the means of realizing them deserve first consideration in restructuring academic government and in reconstituting its membership. New mechanisms are needed to unite the interests and muster the efforts of all constituents of the academic society in the enhancement of the welfare of the whole membership. No one can predict with exactness the benefits that will accrue from bringing students into deliberative and legislative bodies. To what extent such a modification of academic government will help in focusing the discussions and the actions of these organizations on the needed reforms in higher education remains to be seen. It is clear, however, that the reforms that have already occurred in educational institutions and in society at large have abundantly demonstrated that unformalized student intervention in the conventional activities of academic bodies has been effective.

SPECIFIC PREPARATION FOR
GOVERNMENTAL SERVICES

Any discussion of government must consider the meager preparation which most members of the academic community bring to bear on the intricate problems which today urgently demand solution. There is always a time in the history of any profession when its unique lore is passed on through the casual and unsystematized exercises of an apprenticeship. Physicians, lawyers, preachers, architects—all at one time learned their calling in this relatively primitive fashion. Eventually, with the growth of organized knowledge and specialized skills, the members of a guild require applicants for admission to pursue a formal course of institutionalized instruction, at first brief, but eventually long and demanding. Until the present, the practitioners of higher education have typically barely reached the apprenticeship stage. They do, of course, acquire the substantive material of their calling, that is, specialized subject matter. But this is not the peculiar assortment of knowledge and abilities which differentiates teaching from other fields such as the medical profession; the special subject matter of teachers corresponds to anatomy and physiology, which, as every informed person knows, are a very important, but quantitatively small, part of medical education.

There has for a long time been a substantial, but in recent years a swiftly growing, body of literature relevant to the philosophy and purposes of education. This material is not included in "methods courses," the red herrings which the apologists for subject-matter vested interest draw across the path of serious discussion. On the contrary, many of the works are classical treatises with which all persons charged with responsibility for determining the goals and programs of higher education should be familiar. They include the writings of such men as Plato, Aristotle, St. Augustine, Da Feltra, Montaigne, Milton, Ortega y Gasset, Mill, and Whitehead. To these must now be added a large body of relevant current literature produced by scholars in psychology, sociology, education, testing, economics, and government. Of this knowledge some students are no more innocent than the common run of faculty members.

Yet the critical discussions of the entire enterprise of higher education which must be conducted in the days ahead can only proceed in an enlightened manner if the participants in the dialogue are specifically informed about the issues to be decided. The profession can take two steps toward this end. It could and should require all those in training—applicants for graduate degrees—to inform themselves about the mores and the specialized characteristics of their calling through seminars conducted either by the senior members of their chosen disciplines, or by specialists in higher education, or preferably by both in cooperation.

Another device of more long-range significance would be a program of instruction in the history and philosophy of higher education. The world of scholarship has for centuries included studies of the origins, development, significance, and social contributions of every other institution in Western culture—the church, the state, the corporation, and the political parties. The colleges and universities offer courses and often whole programs in these fields. Comparable treatment of higher education as a social institution is relatively scarce. The least the enterprise of higher education could and should do to prepare its future members for an enlightened role would be to offer a solid course of instruction for those who expect to enter the profession. Without such an opportunity to gain the background of essential knowledge and professional orientation, many future discussions of academic issues will be as uninformed and ineffective as they have been in the past. Those students who contemplate becoming active in the government of institutions of higher education should be encouraged to avail themselves, along with their teachers, of such courses to prepare themselves professionally for their duties.

ENABLING STUDENTS TO PARTICIPATE

The discussion of the feasibility of student participation must deal with certain practical problems (in addition to the problems of proportionate representation, selection, and voting rights) which now constitute obstacles difficult to remove. Administrators and students questioned in this study report that some students find membership in academic committees prohibitively burdensome. In the first place they must spend considerable time in gaining an understanding of the kinds of problems various committees deal with, and they must find this time without impairing their scholastic standing or their economic status.

If they are to prove the value of their involvement by discharging their duties creditably, students must acquire the knowledge and experience necessary to come to grips with the important decisions committees make. Anyone familiar with such subjects as institutional purposes, admission requirements, or curriculum content will testify that an extended experience is required to gain insight into the intricacies of the problems these matters involve. A short term in faculty and board committees makes it difficult for anyone to become versed in the esoteric responsibilities involved. Hence even students with the ablest minds and most cooperative spirits may lack the general knowledge of institutions of higher education and their complicated relationship with society essential to sound judgment. The difficulties already encountered even in the institutions which have made the most sincere efforts to bring students into academic councils confirm the need for a longer term than is now common. Unless students' terms extend beyond one year, or unless they can spend hours in specific preparation for their duties, they will normally lack the expertise required for sound judgment. The inadequacy of their knowledge does not preclude students from having a role in academic policy-making. It does imply unusual dedication to the task of acquiring the prerequisite knowledge and the available time to do so.

The other problem which must be solved to make feasible the participation of many students in academic bodies concerns the economic sacrifices they would have to make. The transaction of the normal business of standing committees would drain away valuable time from their studies, but in some cases it would deprive self-supporting students of income without which they could not continue their education. The exorbitant commitment of time has already caused some students, after a rather brief adventuresome period, to question the financial practicability of giving the time necessary for a faithful discharge of their duties.

A clarification of the obligations implied in the phrase "a faithful discharge of their duties" would make committee work less burdensome. If a common misunderstanding of the functions of various groups in academic communities were corrected, a marked reduction could be made in the amount of time members now spend in official activities which ought to be delegated to others. The events of the past several years show that a considerable percentage of faculty members and almost all students fail to recognize the separation of powers and functions necessary for economic and efficient operation in any organization. The entire academic body, or its subgroups, should properly be involved for the deliberative and legislative processes which establish major policies. Only a few designated persons, however, ought to be responsible for putting these policies into effect on a day-to-day basis. Such duties must be assigned to qualified administrators who are given extensive discretionary authority.

In too many institutions the functioning of democratic government is misconceived, and a host of committees spend endless hours reaching decisions which by delegation of authority should have been handled by administrative officers. This prodigal practice involves the misspending of valuable time which faculty members should more properly use in teaching and research, and students in study. Moreover, experience suggests that this wasteful practice often produces no more judicious decisions than those made by administrators operating within established policies. If academic bodies limited their activities to the making of major policy, their work would be less time-consuming and, therefore, more feasible for students.

Even with a proper delimitation of committee functions, however, colleges and universities which admit students to unabridged membership in board and faculty committees will have to take two actions to ensure their effective participation. First, ways will have to be found to enable students to give the necessary time without impairing their scholastic standing. One such device could be a policy under which the institution treated students' participation in the work of a regularly constituted faculty committee as a creditable educational assignment. The intellectual and political experience a student would have as a member of a group dealing with the crucial issues of institutional operation could be as educationally rewarding as course requirements. In fact, such an arrangment might facilitate the efficient conduct of business sometimes delayed by the unavailability of persons with time to gather data and to prepare systematic reports on matters under consideration. Some type of tutorial system could enable students to perform these services without retarding their academic progress. Under controlled circumstances it would be an educationally sound practice to reduce required instructional obligations and to award commensurate academic credit to any student who faithfully discharged his committee responsibilities.

The other barrier which excludes students from academic government is the need for gainful employment during the college years. The dominant purpose of those who attend an institution of higher education should be to pursue their studies. Some of the economically less favored can achieve this goal, however, only by simultaneously earning a substantial part of their living expenses. The American custom of permitting students to earn their way has immeasurably equalized educational opportunity and escalated social mobility, and has thus enhanced the quality of our national life. It is a practice that should be encouraged. Hence, since young people who need current income could only assume committee responsibilities if their consequent loss of income were otherwise offset, they ought to be fairly compensated from institutional resources. Since faculty members and administrative officers are paid for such activities as part of their regular professional responsibilities, a similar arrangement would seem to be equitable for students. In any event if students who are financially self-dependent are to be involved in committee work, some arrangement must be found to pay them.

THE USE OF REASON IN ACADEMIC REFORM

The long intellectual history of Western culture dramatically exhibits modern man's sustained effort to gain an
understanding of himself and the universe around him
through the substitution of reason for emotion, prejudice,
mysticism, and violence. Since the days of the Greeks, men
have laboriously, valiantly, and often sacrificially striven
for the right to think and speak in accordance with their
convictions and their conscience. Millions have suffered
and died to gain and to preserve the privilege of resolving
social problems through unrestricted and open discussion.
Philosophers through the ages from Plato to Whitehead
have employed and advocated the use of rational, systematic, logical thought in the expansion of knowledge and in
the conduct of human affairs. In the main the stoutest
advocates of freedom of assembly, speech, and action have
also been the staunchest defenders of the principle of
abiding by the final decision of the majority. American
centers of learning ought to preserve, enhance, and propa-
gate these intellectual traditions not only in their instructional programs but in the behavior of their members and
in the conduct of their affairs.

Without detracting from the beneficial social and academic reforms achieved by a relatively small percentage
of activists, several factors which will determine the long-
run influence of students on educational policy should be
considered.

First, although much overdue reform in higher education has been *initiated,* departures from established policies
have by no means been firmly fixed in the practices of
colleges and universities. The growing resistance to tumult
and coercion among trustees, administrators, faculty members, and students themselves, to say nothing of the general

public, suggests that further and more lasting reconstruction of goals and processes will be accomplished only through rational discussion of the issues on which the various members of the academic society hold a wide range of views.

Second, all but a very few of those in the academic fraternity who are the most ardent supporters of student activist goals now recognize that institutions committed to the pursuit of truth through the unrestricted exercise of reason must be able to assure their members freedom to carry on their intellectual activities in an atmosphere of calm. The concern expressed by some 800 members of the Columbia University faculty in their 1969 statement, "The University as a Sanctuary of Academic Freedom," is typical of the fear among academics that a continuation of disruptions, such as those at Columbia in 1968, would inevitably destroy the spiritual essence of the educational establishment if not its material manifestation.

The great majority of reformers rejects the theory that the entire establishment must be tumbled down before desirable reconstruction can begin. In fact they consider the institutions of higher education and their members the best and perhaps the only agency a free society has for the preservation of its liberties and for the improvement of its common life. Without denying that students can help in achieving needed reforms in higher education, America's most distinguished historian has issued a warning against the perils involved in misconceiving its purpose or disrupting its essential services. In this vein Henry Steele Commager has declared:

> The University is the most honorable and the least corrupt institution in American life. It is, with the church, the one institution that associates us with the past and the future,

the one institution that has, through all of our history, served or tried to serve, the interests of the whole of mankind and the interests of truth.

No other institution can perform the functions which the university performs, no other can fill the place which it has for so long filled, and with such intellectual and moral affluence.

If we destroy the university we will destroy a unique institution. As the integrity of civilization depends in part on the university, we will be dealing an irreparable blow to a civilization now in moral peril.[12]

If students are to have a voice in shaping the policies and the practices of these centers of learning, they will have to take their places on academic bodies with a commitment to the concept of resolving differences of opinion and solving practical problems through the free expression of ideas and the exercise of the vote. They must also be ready after they have exercised their rights to accept the decision of the majority. If the movements of academic bodies seem too sluggish, as they customarily are, they can be accelerated by a continuance of the public protests, the free speech, the freedom of assembly guaranteed under the First Amendment. In many respects, students are best equipped by knowledge, compassionate feeling, and vigorous spirit to accomplish long-overdue reforms. But they can expect the desirable changes they bring about to become permanent only if the other members of society can be persuaded of their value through the presentation of reliable fact and logical argument. This is the democratic way, the most likely alternative to which is the dictatorial suppression of all minority opinion.

[12] Henry Steele Commager, "Universities Can and Must Be Saved from Destruction," *The Philadelphia Inquirer,* September 7, 1969, sec. 7, p. 1.

CONCLUSIONS

The evidence indicates that revolutionary changes are occurring in the structure of government in American colleges and universities. Some of the most significant of these alterations in practices which have existed for centuries are related to the role of students in the academic bodies which determine the purposes and practices of higher education. Hardly any institution remains untouched by the activities of students aimed at gaining a voice in major policy-making decisions.

The facts clearly indicate, however, that institutional progress in academic reconstruction is quite uneven. At one end of the scale are some institutions which have added an influential number of students to all major committees and have given them the full complement of parliamentary privileges enjoyed by faculty members, administrative officers, and trustees. But the institutions in this category constitute a negligible percentage of the whole. The majority have added only a few students, often only one or two, to some committees and frequently have given them merely the status of disputants, pleaders, or observers. At the other end of the scale are a few institutions in which students have yet to gain any formal role in academic deliberative or

103

legislative bodies. Neither experience nor informed opinion
has yet definitively established in which bodies students
should have membership, what proportion of the total they
should be, or how they should be selected. There is, however, a growing volume of opinion that students should have
the right to be involved in all the agencies which determine
major institutional policies, and in particular that they
should be admitted to committees which fix the purposes
of the institution, design the educational program for their
achievement, and organize and control other activities
which shape the general character of the academic community. Moreover, to be effective and to assure their constituents that they speak for the whole student body, these
representatives ought to be chosen by their own associates.

The specific structure and the political processes of the
academic government of the future must yet be determined. But that the government ought to be structured
around the concept of community can hardly be denied. At
present rather discrete social groups—the trustees, the administrative staff, the faculty members, and the students—
legislate on, or otherwise influence, some aspects of policy.
For years this separatism of powers, supported by law or
custom, has been generally accepted by all groups in the
academic community, but for decades there have been dis-
sident opinions on the structure and allocation of responsibilities. Recently these dissenting views have become more
vocal and widespread. There is a growing opinion that the
differences which have arisen among the constituent groups
are no longer reconcilable through conventional procedures.
Moreover, the differences remain a potential source of misunderstanding and severely disruptive conflict.

Many believe that until students have a direct and
officially recognized means of expressing their views on

these matters the academic society will be subject to recurrent disorders which will handicap the students' own education and reduce the social benefits which should flow from it. Hence thoughtful persons are convinced that the students' views on the changes that need to be made in American society and in higher education must be brought into official discussions of academic bodies, not as the recommendations of outsiders or supplicants, but as the expression of regularly constituted members of a community who have a right to participate in the activities of their government.

Where students have been fully involved in academic government, they have typically discharged their responsibilities with effectiveness and with dignity. The few American institutions with decades of practice, and the Canadian universities with considerable but shorter experience, with few exceptions authenticate the workability and the value of student participation. Their experience also suggests that a governmental structure which assembles all the constituent parties in some organization like a senate, including the board, the administrators, the faculty, and the students in policy discussion *ab initio* is better than one which provides for the reconciliation of opposing views after the constituent groups have taken independent action. What is required now is large-scale experimentation to find by trial and evaluation those structures and processes of academic government which best fit our traditions and the emerging conditions of American life. All citizens owe a debt of gratitude to the American Assembly on University Goals and Governance for mobilizing the vast resources of academic and lay organizations in an effort to make the needed reforms with a minimum of disruption to the ongoing processes of higher education.

APPENDIX

STUDENT PARTICIPATION IN SELECTED
POLICY-MAKING BODIES OF COLLEGES AND
UNIVERSITIES: FIVE TABLES

1. OVERALL

Policy-Making Body	Percentage of Responding Colleges and Universities Having Student Participation
Board of trustees	
Voting membership	2.7
Any participation[a]	20.0
Board of trustees committees[a]	10.6[b]
One or more faculty committees[a]	88.3
Faculty executive committee	
Voting membership	17.9
Any participation[a]	22.7
Faculty curriculum committee	
Voting membership	46.1
Any participation[a]	57.8
Faculty committee on faculty selection, promotion, and tenure	
Voting membership	3.3
Any participation[a]	4.7

(Continued on next page)

1. OVERALL (continued)

Policy-Making Body	Percentage of Responding Colleges and Universities Having Student Participation
Other faculty committees[a]	83.3
Admissions[a]	17.5
Library[a]	31.2
Planning[a]	9.7
Public events, lectures, etc.[a]	29.1
Discipline[a]	18.6
Student life[a]	34.3
Usable responses received (N)	875
Percentage response	65.4

SOURCE: Responses of 875 colleges and universities to questionnaire mailed September 1969.

[a] Includes both voting membership and non-voting participation.

[b] Includes 42 institutions (4.8% of the total) in which students were reported not to sit with the board, but nevertheless to sit with one or more of the board committees.

2. BY HIGHEST LEVEL OF INSTITUTIONAL OFFERING

Policy-Making Body	Percentage of Responding Colleges and Universities Having Student Participation		
	Highest Level of Offering[a]		
	II	III	IV
Board of trustees			
Voting membership	2.2	3.7	2.1
Any participation[b]	18.9	21.2	20.8
Board of trustees committees[b,c]	10.3	11.4	10.4
One or more faculty committees[b]	86.5	89.7	93.1
Faculty executive committee			
Voting membership	19.1	17.2	16.0
Any participation[b]	23.6	23.4	19.4
Faculty curriculum committee			
Voting membership	49.4	48.7	31.9
Any participation[b]	60.5	59.7	47.9
Faculty committee on faculty selection, promotion, and tenure			
Voting membership	2.9	3.7	4.2
Any participation[b]	4.0	5.1	5.6
Other faculty committees[b]	82.5	84.2	86.1
Admissions[b]	17.8	17.2	17.4
Library[b]	32.1	28.9	33.3
Planning[b]	9.9	7.7	12.5
Public events, lectures, etc.[b]	30.3	30.0	25.7
Discipline[b]	16.6	21.2	20.8
Student life[b]	34.4	38.1	28.5
Usable responses received (N)	445	273	144
Percentage response	62.8	66.9	67.3

(Continued on next page)

SOURCE: Responses of 862 colleges and universities to questionnaire mailed September 1969 and *Education Directory, 1967-68: Part 3, Higher Education.*

a The following classifications, taken from Part 3 of the *Education Directory,* have been employed:

II. Institutions offering only the bachelor's and/or first professional degree.

III. Institutions offering the master's and/or second professional degree.

IV. Institutions offering the doctor of philosophy and equivalent degrees.

b Includes both voting membership and non-voting participation.

c Includes the following numbers of institutions which reported that students did not sit with the board, but indicated that students did sit with one or more board committees:

Level of Offering	Number of Institutions	Percentage of Total Usable Responses
II	19	4.3
III	13	4.8
IV	7	4.9

3. BY INSTITUTIONAL ENROLLMENT, 1967-68

	Percentage of Responding Colleges and Universities Having Student Participation				
	Institutional Enrollment				
Policy-Making Body	0-499	500-999	1,000-1,999	2,000-4,999	5,000 and over
Board of trustees					
Voting membership	4.9	2.5	2.8	1.3	2.7
Any participation[a]	13.6	14.9	24.3	18.6	25.1
Board of trustees committees[a,b]	3.9	12.9	14.0	12.8	7.0
One or more faculty committees[a]	69.9	87.1	93.5	91.0	92.0
Faculty executive committee					
Voting membership	12.6	19.8	20.1	13.5	19.8
Any participation[a]	19.4	24.7	23.8	18.6	24.6
Faculty curriculum committee					
Voting membership	33.0	51.5	55.6	46.2	37.4
Any participation[a]	42.7	62.9	68.7	58.3	48.7
Faculty committee on faculty selection, promotion, and tenure					
Voting membership	1.9	2.0	2.8	3.8	5.9
Any participation[a]	4.9	4.0	3.3	5.1	6.4
Other faculty committees[a]	66.0	81.7	89.7	87.8	84.0
Admissions[a]	9.7	15.8	27.1	14.7	13.9
Library[a]	22.3	33.2	35.5	26.3	31.6
Planning[a]	8.7	9.9	8.4	7.1	13.4
Public events, lectures, etc.[a]	15.5	30.2	34.1	34.0	25.7
Discipline[a]	10.7	15.3	18.7	25.0	20.9
Student life[a]	23.3	35.1	38.8	35.3	36.9
Usable responses received (N)	103	202	214	156	187
Percentage response	57.9	66.0	65.0	67.0	65.8

(Continued on next page)

SOURCE: Responses of 862 colleges and universities to question-naire mailed September 1969 and *Education Directory, 1967-68: Part 3, Higher Education.*

a Includes both voting membership and non-voting participation.
b Includes the following numbers of institutions which reported that students did not sit with the board, but indicated that students did sit with one or more board committees:

Enrollment	Number of Institutions	Percentage of Total Usable Responses
0- 499	2	1.9
500- 999	11	5.4
1,000-1,999	12	5.6
2,000-4,999	10	6.4
5,000 and over	6	3.2

4. BY TYPE OF INSTITUTIONAL SUPPORT

Policy-Making Body	*Percentage of Responding Colleges and Universities Having Student Participation*			
	Type of Supporting Body			
	Roman Catholic	*Religious Other than Roman Catholic*	*Private*	*Public*
Board of trustees				
Voting membership	1.8	2.4	2.1	4.3
Any participation[a]	9.8	24.5	15.2	27.7
Board of trustees committees[a,b]	9.8	14.2	13.5	6.3
One or more faculty committees[a]	89.0	91.5	79.3	94.1
Faculty executive committee				
Voting membership	22.7	18.4	13.1	19.0
Any participation[a]	27.6	22.6	16.5	25.3
Faculty curriculum committee				
Voting membership	57.1	51.4	38.0	43.1
Any participation[a]	66.9	61.8	52.3	54.2
Faculty committee on faculty selection, promotion, and tenure				
Voting membership	4.9	1.9	3.0	3.6
Any participation[a]	5.5	3.3	4.6	4.7
Other faculty committees[a]	84.0	86.3	73.8	89.7
Admissions[a]	16.0	20.3	21.1	12.3
Library[a]	32.5	30.7	26.6	34.4
Planning[a]	6.1	10.4	7.6	13.8
Public events, lectures, etc.[a]	22.1	34.0	25.7	32.8
Discipline[a]	15.3	13.2	17.7	25.7
Student life[a]	34.4	43.4	27.8	35.2
Usable responses received (N)	163	212	237	253
Percentage response	63.9	62.7	70.5	62.6

(Continued on next page)

SOURCE: Responses of 865 colleges and universities to question-
naire mailed September 1969 and *Education Directory, 1967-68:
Part 3, Higher Education.*

a Includes both voting membership and non-voting participation.
b Includes the following numbers of institutions which reported that
students did not sit with the board, but indicated that students did
sit with one or more board committees:

Type of Supporting Body	Number of Institutions	Percentage of Total Usable Responses
Roman Catholic	6	3.7
Religious other than Roman Catholic	12	5.7
Private	18	7.6
Public	5	2.0

5. BY ACCREDITING REGION

	Percentage of Responding Colleges and Universities Having Student Participation					
	Accrediting Region					
Policy-Making Body	Middle States	New England	North Central	Northwest	Southern	Western
Board of trustees						
Voting membership	1.6	16.9	0.3	4.5	2.1	1.8
Any participation[a]	14.1	29.9	22.3	20.5	18.7	17.5
Board of trustees committees[a,b]	12.4	16.9	10.0	15.9	6.7	8.8
One or more faculty committees[a]	84.3	89.6	87.1	95.5	90.2	94.7
Faculty executive committee						
Voting membership	16.2	18.2	20.1	15.9	18.7	10.5
Any participation[a]	21.1	18.2	25.7	20.5	22.8	19.3
Faculty curriculum committee						
Voting membership	42.2	45.5	50.5	38.6	44.6	45.6
Any participation[a]	54.6	62.3	60.5	47.7	57.0	57.9
Faculty committee on faculty selection, promotion, and tenure						
Voting membership	6.5	2.6	2.8	4.5	1.0	3.5
Any participation[a]	8.6	5.2	3.8	4.5	1.6	7.0
Other faculty committees[a]	78.4	83.1	83.7	90.9	83.9	89.5
Admissions[a]	20.5	28.6	15.7	11.4	16.1	12.3
Library[a]	31.9	32.5	32.6	36.4	27.5	28.1
Planning[a]	10.3	11.7	9.1	15.9	6.2	15.8
Public events, lectures, etc.[a]	25.4	28.6	33.5	27.3	28.5	21.1
Discipline[a]	18.4	23.4	16.0	29.5	19.2	17.5
Student life[a]	30.8	39.0	42.0	29.5	24.4	33.3
Usable responses received (N)	185	77	319	44	193	57
Percentage response	71.2	59.7	68.1	75.9	58.0	65.5

(Continued on next page)

SOURCE: Responses of 875 colleges and universities to question-naire mailed September 1969 and *Accredited Institutions of Higher Education,* September 1968.

a Includes both voting membership and non-voting participation.
b Includes the following numbers of institutions which reported that students did not sit with the board, but indicated that students did sit with one or more board committees:

Accrediting Region	Number of Institutions	Percentage of Total Usable Responses
Middle States	16	8.6
New England	6	7.8
North Central	9	2.8
Northwest	2	4.5
Southern	6	3.1
Western	2	3.5

BIBLIOGRAPHY

Aceto, Thomas D. "Student Participation in Policy Making and the Use of Direct Action at the Mid-West Committee on Institutional Cooperation Universities." Ph.D. dissertation, Syracuse University, 1967.

Ad Hoc Committee on the Role of Students in the Government of the University. "Report to the University Committee." Madison: University of Wisconsin, 1968.

Alexander, William M. "Rethinking Student Government for Larger Universities." *Journal of Higher Education,* January 1969, pp. 39-46.

Auerbach, Carl A. "Memo to the Members of the University Faculty on the Subject of the Task Force Recommendations on Student Representation in the University Senate and Campus Assemblies." Minneapolis: University of Minnesota, February 24, 1969.

Babbidge, Homer D., Jr. *Eighth Annual Faculty Convocation.* Storrs: University of Connecticut, November 6, 1969.

Benovich, Joseph B. and others. *Report of the President's Committee on Student Involvement in the University.* Cleveland, Ohio: Cleveland State University, May 16, 1969.

Blair, Carolyn L. *All-College Council at Maryville College.* Maryville, Tenn.: Maryville College, 1969.

Bloustein, Edward J. "The New Student and His Role in American Colleges." *Liberal Education*, October 1968, pp. 345-364.

Boren, James E. "Cooperative Government at the University of Minnesota." In *Role and Structure of Student Government*, edited by Mary Meehan. Washington, D.C.: U. S. National Student Association, 1966.

Bowles, W. Donald. "Student Participation in Academic Governance." *Educational Record*, Summer 1968, pp. 257-262.

Brewster, Kingman, Jr. *The Report of the President. Yale University: 1967-68*. New Haven: Yale University, September 1968.

Brunson, May A. "Student Involvement in University Governance: Sense or Nonsense?" *Journal of the National Association of Women Deans and Counselors*, Summer 1969, pp. 169-175.

Caffrey, John, ed. *The Future Academic Community: Continuity and Change*. Washington, D.C.: American Council on Education, 1969.

"Campus Government at Stanford." *Universities*, October 12, 1968, p. 330.

Carr, Alden J. *Student Participation in College Policy Determination and Administration*. AACTE Study Series No. 4. Washington, D.C.: American Association of Colleges for Teacher Education, 1969.

Charter and By-Laws of the Spring Hill College Senate. Mobile: Spring Hill College, 1969.

The College Senate. By-Laws. Lancaster, Pa.: Franklin and Marshall College, November 26, 1969.

Commager, Henry Steele. "Universities Can and Must Be Saved from Destruction." *The Philadelphia Inquirer*, September 7, 1969, sec. 7, p. 1.

Committee on the Student in Higher Education. *The Student in Higher Education*. New Haven, Conn.: Hazen Foundation, January 1968.

"Constitution of the Yeshiva College Senate." New York: Yeshiva College, 1969.

Constructive Changes to Ease Campus Tensions. Washington, D.C.: Office of Institutional Research, National Association of State Universities and Land-Grant Colleges, 1968.

"Conversations." In *Student Participation in University Decisions: Where Are We, Where Are We Going in the Student Movement?* Philadelphia: ARA-Slater School & College Services, 1969.

Davis, John B., Jr. "A Survey of Practices Related to Student Membership on Academic Committees." A report for the Faculty Senate Committee on Committees. Greenville, N.C.: East Carolina University, 1969.

Demerath, Nicholas J.; Stephens, Richard W.; and Taylor, R. Robb. *Power, Presidents, and Professors.* New York and London: Basic Books, 1967.

Desmond, Richard. "Faculty and Student Frustrations Shaping the Future of the University." *AAUP Bulletin,* March 1969, pp. 23-26.

Duff, James and Berdahl, Robert O. *University Government in Canada.* Report of a Commission sponsored by the Canadian Association of University Teachers and the Association of Universities and Colleges of Canada. Toronto: University of Toronto Press, 1966.

Duster, Troy. "Student Interests, Student Power, and the Swedish Experience." *The American Behavioral Scientist,* May 1968, pp. 21-27.

"Final Report of the Antioch College Commission on Governance." Washington, D. C.: U. S. National Student Association, June 1968.

Foote, Caleb; Mayer, Henry; and associates. *The Culture of the University: Governance and Education.* San Francisco: Jossey-Bass, 1968.

Footlick, Jerrold K. "A Testing by Protest." *The College Scene Now.* Silver Spring, Md.: Dow Jones, 1967.

Frankel, Charles. "Student Power: The Rhetoric and The Possibilities." *Saturday Review,* November 2, 1968, pp. 23-25.

Frick, Ivan E. "Reflections on Participatory Democracy." *Liberal Education,* May 1969, pp. 262-271.

Governance Report. New York: Queens College, City University of New York, November 1969.

"Governing a College: Curriculum, yes; Social life, no!" *College Management,* May 1969, pp. 53-54.

"Governing a College: How Much Should Students Have to Say?" *College Management,* May 1969, pp. 30-39.

"Governing a College: The Pros and Cons of Student Involvement." *College Management,* May 1969, pp. 40-44.

"Governing a College: A Unified Command." *College Management,* May 1969, pp. 48-49.

"Governing a College: Whose Man Is the Chancellor?" *College Management,* May 1969, pp. 56-60.

"Governing Boards: Trustees Strive to Close Generation Gap —But Not by Opening Board to Students." *College and University Business,* April 1969, p. 24.

"Government of the University." In *The Study of Education at Stanford. Report to the University.* Stanford, Calif.: Stanford University, February 1969.

Hallberg, Edmond C. "An Academic Congress: A Direction in University Governance." *Phi Delta Kappan,* May 1969, pp. 538-540.

Hartnett, Rodney T. *College and University Trustees: Their Backgrounds, Roles and Educational Attitudes.* Princeton, N.J.: Educational Testing Service, 1969.

Hefferlin, JB Lon. *Dynamics of Academic Reform.* San Francisco: Jossey-Bass, 1969.

Heffner, Ray L. "The Student Voice in Institutional Policy." *AGB Reports,* February 1968, pp. 3-10.

Hekhuis, Louis Frederick. "A Comparison of the Perceptions of Students and Faculty at Michigan State University with Respect to Student Participation in University Policy Formulation." Ph.D. dissertation, Michigan State University, 1967.

Henderson, Algo D. *Policies and Practices in Higher Education.* New York: Harper and Brothers, 1960.

———. "The Administrator/Student Conflict." *Administrative Law Review,* November 1968, pp. 65-77.

Hodgkinson, Harold L. *Governance and Factions—Who Decides Who Decides?* Berkeley: Center for Research and Development in Higher Education, University of California, July 1968.

————. "Students and an Intellectual Community." *Educational Record*, Fall 1968, pp. 398-406.

————. "Student Participation in Campus Governance." A paper presented at the AERA Conference, Los Angeles, Calif., 1969.

————. "Student Protest—An Institutional and National Profile." *Teachers College Record*, May 1970, pp. 537-555.

"Issues in University Governance." A report to the Ford Foundation on the Summer Colloquium on University Governance. New York: Institute of Higher Education, Department of Higher and Adult Education, Teachers College, Columbia University, September 1968.

Jenks, R. Stephen. *The Student Role in Faculty Selection, Evaluation and Retention*. Washington, D.C.: National Association of State Universities and Land Grant Colleges, November 10, 1969.

Jenks, R. Stephen and others. *Report of the Committee on Government Organization*. Durham: University of New Hampshire, March 6, 1969.

Johnstone, Bruce D. "The Student and His Power." *Journal of Higher Education*, March 1969, pp. 205-218.

Joughin, Louis. "The Role of the Student in College and University Government." In *Symposium on Academic Freedom and Responsibility*. Los Angeles: California State College, May 22, 1968.

Kerlinger, Fred N. "Student Participation in University Educational Decision Making." *Teachers College Record*, October 1968, pp. 45-51.

Knock, Gary H. and others. *The Report of the Commission on Student Participation in University Life*. Oxford, Ohio: Miami University, September 1969.

Leadership and Responsibility on the Changing Campus: Who's in Charge Here? Papers presented at the AASCU 8th Annual Meeting. Washington, D.C.: American Association of State Colleges and Universities, November 1968.

Lunn, Harry H., Jr. *The Student's Role in College Policy Making.* A report prepared for the Commission on Student Personnel. Washington, D.C.: American Council on Education, 1957.

Macneil, Ian. "The President's Commission on Student Involvement in Decision-Making. A Comment." Mimeographed [ERIC reading list], 1969.

Main, Jeremy. "The 'Square' Universities Are Rolling, Too." *Fortune,* January 1969, pp. 104ff.

Marchese, Theodore J. "Student Participation in Plans Is No Longer a Question of Whether, but How? *College and University Business,* August 1969, pp. 37-38.

Martin, Warren Bryan. "Student Participation in Academic Governance." *Current Issues in Higher Education.* Washington, D.C.: American Association for Higher Education, 1967.

McDonough, John R. "The Role of Students in Governing the University." *AGB Reports,* April 1968, pp. 24-31.

McGehee, Nan E. "Faculty and Students, or Faculty Versus Students." Mimeographed [ERIC reading list], 1969.

Meehan, Mary, ed. *Role and Structure of Student Government.* Washington, D.C.: U. S. National Student Association, 1966.

Milton, Ohmer. *Survey of Faculty Views on Student Participation in Decision Making.* Final Report Project No. 7-D-037. Washington, D.C.: U. S. Department of Health, Education and Welfare, Office of Education, Bureau of Research, May 1968.

Mitau, Theodore. "Student Participation in Campus Government." A paper presented at Student Convocation, St. Cloud College. St. Cloud, Minn., February 18, 1969.

Morison, Robert S. *The President's Commission on Student Involvement in Decision-Making: The Chairman's Report.* Ithaca: Cornell University, June 11, 1969.

Morris, Arval A. "Student Participation in University Decision Making." Mimeographed [ERIC reading list], 1969.

Muston, Ray A. "Governance Changes Are Catching Colleges by Surprise, National Survey Shows." *College and University Business,* July 1969, pp. 29-31.

Orcutt, John. "How Deans and Students See It." In *Focus on Action: A Handbook for Developing Junior Colleges,* edited by Selden Menefee and John Orcutt. Washington, D.C.: American Association of Junior Colleges, May 1969.

Ostar, Allan W. and Otten, Jane. "Fresh Developments at State Higher Education Institutions." *School and Society,* January 20, 1968, pp. 48-50.

Powell, Robert S., Jr. "Participation is Learning." *Saturday Review,* January 10, 1970, pp. 56ff.

A Progress Report by the Committee on University Governance. Boca Raton: Florida Atlantic University, May 6, 1969.

A Proposal to Establish the Council of the Princeton University Community. A Report of the Special Committee on the Structure of the University. Princeton, N.J.: Princeton University, May 1969.

"Proposed Alterations in the Governance of the University." Stanford, Calif.: American Association of University Professors, Stanford University Chapter, October 3, 1968.

Proposed Codes with Commentary: Student Conduct and Discipline Proceedings in a University Setting. New York: New York University School of Law, August 1968.

Proposed Constitution for a University Senate of Morehead State University. Recommendations of the Special Committee on University Government. Morehead, Ky.: Morehead State University, May 20, 1969.

Rashdall, Hastings. *The Universities of Europe in the Middle Ages.* Vol. 1. London: Oxford University Press, 1936.

Recommendations for the Governance of Wesleyan University. Middletown, Conn.: Wesleyan University, September 6, 1969.

Report of the University of Minnesota Task Force on Student Representation. Minneapolis: University of Minnesota, January 2, 1969.

Revised Report of the Committee on University Governance. The Executive Committee of the Committee on University Governance. Binghamton: State University of New York, March 14, 1969.

Richardson, Richard C., Jr. "Recommendations on Student Rights and Freedoms: Some Procedural Considerations for the Two-Year College." *Junior College Journal,* February 1969, pp. 34-44.

Rudolph, Frederick. *The American College and University: A History.* New York: Alfred A. Knopf, 1962.

————. "Neglect of Students as a Historical Tradition." In *The College and the Student,* edited by Lawrence E. Dennis and Joseph F. Kauffman. Washington, D.C.: American Council on Education, 1966.

Schwartz, Edward. *Joint Statement on the Academic Freedom of Students. A Summary and Analysis.* Washington, D.C.: U. S. National Student Association, 1967.

Schwartz, Edward, ed. *Student Power. A Collection of Readings.* Washington, D.C.: U. S. National Student Association, January 1969.

Schwebel, Robert. "Wakening Our Sleepy Universities: Student Involvement in Curriculum Change." *Teachers College Record,* October 1968, pp. 31-43.

Second Interim Report to the Trustees of Columbia University. New York: Columbia University, March 17, 1969.

Senate Code. Lawrence: The University of Kansas, December 20, 1968.

Shoben, Edward Joseph, Jr. "Student and University Governance: A Preliminary Sketch." Mimeographed [ERIC reading list], 1969.

Smith, Thomas A. "The Trinity College Council . . . Experiment in Collegiality." *Trinity Alumni Magazine,* Summer 1969, pp. 18-22, 47-49.

Sparzo, Frank J. "Facing the Issues of Student Unrest." *School and Society,* October 26, 1968, pp. 359-361.

Splete, Allen P. *An Interim Report on Student Representation in the Academic Community at Syracuse University.* New York: Syracuse University, May 1969.

Student Participation in University Government." A study paper prepared for the Committee of Presidents of Universities of Ontario by its Subcommittee on Research and Planning. Toronto: University of Toronto Press, 1968.

Student Power at the University of Massachusetts. A Case Study. Amherst: Massachusetts University, April 1969.

Third Interim Report to the Trustees of Columbia University. New York: Columbia University, May 12, 1969.

Vaccaro, Louis C. and Covert, James T., eds. *Student Freedom.* New York: Teachers College Press, Columbia University, 1969.

Werdell, Philip P. "An Open Letter to Educators on Student Participation in Decision Making." Washington, D.C.: U. S. National Student Association, 1968.

Who's in Charge? A Special Report. Baltimore, Maryland: Editorial Projects for Education, 1969.

"Why Students Act That Way—A Gallup Study." *U. S. News and World Report,* June 2, 1969, pp. 34-35.

Wilson, Logan. "Protest Politics and Campus Reform." *Administrative Law Review,* November 1968, pp. 45-64.

Wilson, Robert C. and Gaff, Jerry G. "Student Voice—Faculty Response." In *The Research Reporter,* pp. 1-4. Berkeley: Center for Research and Development in Higher Education, University of California, 1969.

Wofford, Harris. "New and Old Actors in Institutional Decision Making." *Current Campus Issues.* Cambridge, Mass.: University Consultants, Inc., 1969.